PLAYING WITH FIRE . . .

He got up off the bed and was moving toward her with a sureness that showed he was certainly not hopelessly drunk.

"What are you doing here, Florian?" she asked fearfully.

"You know what I am doing here."

Yes, she did . . . and no, she didn't. This was what she wanted, wasn't it? Utterly confused, she felt the tears trickle under the silk mask. His hands were on her shoulders now, stroking her throat and her nearly exposed breasts.

"I must tell you, Estelle, I intend to have you. You have played me for a while and here I am, as you planned."

"Florian, I planned nothing! I only wanted to flirt with you, to make them jealous! . . ."

He pulled her against him now, holding her tightly around the waist, forcing her head back with the urgency of his kisses. She felt her legs part, his hands start to pull at her skirt, ripping the flimsy fabric from her . . . Desperately, she tried to hold him off, pushing against his chest, pleading with him.

"No, no – this is wrong, wicked – this is for marriage – let me go, please let me go!"

Also by the same author, and available from Coronet:

ANGEL IN BABYLON
TURN OF THE CENTURY

Dark Liaisons

Jill Downie

CORONET BOOKS
Hodder and Stoughton

The characters and situations in this book are entirely imaginary and bear no relation to any real person or actual happening.

First published in Canada in 1985 by PaperJacks Ltd.

Coronet edition 1988

British Library C.I.P.

Downie, Jill
Dark liaisons.
I. Title
813′.54[F] PS3554.093/

ISBN 0 340 41896 6

Printed and bound in Great Britain for Hodder and Stoughton Paperbacks, a division of Hodder and Stoughton Ltd., Mill Road, Dunton Green, Sevenoaks, Kent TN13 2YA.
(Editorial Office: 47 Bedford Square, London WC1B 3DP) by Cox & Wyman Ltd., Reading

For my brothers, Richard and Christopher Green
And with *hommage* to Choderlos de Laclos

Chapter One

THE HOUSE IN WHICH SHE HAD BEEN REBORN three months ago stood on the rocky heights above the harbor of Saint Peter Port. The other houses of the town stretched around and about across the cliffside, but none disturbed her view of the harbor or the channel that lay between Guernsey and the islands of Herm and Jethou.

From her bedroom window the beauty of the scene was hers for the asking. She was apart, a princess in a tower, but the noises of the port and the town market, Les Halles, were carried to her eyrie on the breeze.

"Princess in a tower." Luc — old, faithful Luc, kept on beyond his usefulness — had called her that once. Celestine had given him a look of such powerful anger it was a wonder he had not turned to stone. Defiantly, Luc had replied in patois, but his was the patois of Torteval and Estelle could not understand what he said. All she had grasped was Celestine's vehement response: *"Il faut savèr ouïr, véer, et se taire!"* One must know how to hear, see, and be silent. Thus old Luc became part of the conspiracy of silence that surrounded her.

The young woman bent her head over the writing-desk and wrote:

"My name is Estelle Gastineau. I only know that because I have been told it is so. I came into existence in this room about three months ago. I am the creation of what others tell me."

Estelle looked at the hand holding the pen before returning it to the inkwell. The hands of a stranger, becoming more familiar now after three months, well tended, a square palm with slim fingers that tipped crookedly at the end. She dipped her pen into the ink and wrote: "I am obviously right-handed and remember how to read and write. I can also write in French — easily, but perhaps not as effortlessly as in English. It must be because both languages are used on the island."

A gust of wind from the open window made the oil lamp suddenly flicker and flare up. Estelle stood up and pulled the curtain away from it, then leaned over the desk, her attention caught by the beautiful spare lines of Herm and Jethou in the last of the fading light.

"But it's not the French of these islands," she murmured. "They neither write it nor speak as I do."

Panic filled her, as it did when she tried to force memory to return. When she let things flow and the flashes of remembrance came, brief and disconnected as they were, they did not always disturb her. Celestine had warned her, "Don't try to remember. Why should you? You are young, *belle fille,* with a life ahead of you. Allow it to disappear, or reappear as it chooses. *Pûs de broue que de travâs* — you push and it will only be slower."

Celestine's was the first face Estelle remembered seeing three months ago. Celestine Falla had been Estelle's nurse. At least, that was what Celestine had told her. Estelle didn't doubt it, because she had instinctively reached out from the bed and clutched Celestine's hand when she heard the words *"ma petite."*

"Nou-nou," Estelle had said, like a baby.

"You used to call me that." There had been tears in the old woman's eyes. *Nourrice* — nurse — *nou-nou.* It made sense, but in her heart she accepted it, too. And this woman, her closest link to reality, believed silence was best and that Estelle must remember for herself. "And why should you want to, anyway?" Celestine would add alarmingly.

Estelle had been told that she had had a dreadful experience that caused her loss of memory. She had been brought back to Le Refuge, the home of her ancestors — but from where had not been specified. She had been given the dower wing as her own, with Celestine to look after her.

The main part of Le Refuge dated back to the end of the seventeenth century, but the dower wing had been added only fifty years ago, around 1800, when the facade of the building had been remodeled in the Georgian style. It had a separate garden, kitchen, and bedrooms. There was a door upstairs and down that connected to the main house, where her aunt and uncle lived with their four children.

So thick were the walls that sounds of their existence rarely penetrated. Estelle was aware of them only when she joined them occasionally for a meal. Sometimes, she would look up from her plate and catch her aunt's eyes upon her. In them she would read curiosity, amazement, even horror.

Estelle was, however, treated with politeness and consideration. Her uncle was her mother's brother. Her mother had been very beautiful, the pride of one of the "sixty families," the élite of Guernsey, and had gone to the mainland to marry. She had died shortly after giving birth to Estelle, and the infant had been returned to the island for her upbringing. That much Estelle had been told.

In the past three months of her renewed existence she had learned only that the Gastineaus were monied, pious, and part of the island aristocracy. Amid comfort, if not luxury, they lived their lives bounded by island custom and habit, with few books, little conversation, fewer pleasures. Yet they appeared content with their lot. It was she alone who seemed to disturb the pattern, bringing doubt and surprise into their circumspect existence.

Estelle swung away from the window, bracing herself against

the desk as her head throbbed. It often did if she moved suddenly. She had been told it was a result of the "bad experience" and that it would pass. She had the impression her kinsfolk would not be in the least disturbed if she remained an invalid for a long while. It separated her from the outside world and from awkward questions which she could not, and they did not care, to answer.

And in that sudden movement came one of the flashes of recall. She saw, not this room with its solid, substantial furniture, but another: a coffer and cabinets of coromandel lacquer — she knew they were, but how did she know that — a large writing desk with a surface of green Siberian malachite, tapestries on the wall, an English needlework carpet of floral sprays, a painted ceiling. No oil lamps here, but candelabra in stands of tortoise-shell and silver. Estelle knew this room, knew knew it well, heard voices drifting through it — English, langorous, drawling, caressing her with words, with . . . .

She came back, surfacing into the present, to the sound of Celestine's anxious voice. "Estelle! *Qu'est-qu'tu as?* What have you been doing?"

She was on the floor, with Celestine crouching over her, wiping her face with a damp cloth. "Why do you write? Why do these things? Look what happens! Ah, forget, let it be! How many times must I tell you?"

"It wasn't the writing, it just happened. A room came back to me. . . . Listen."

Celestine listened impatiently, brushing aside the recollection before Estelle had finished.

"That imagination of yours! Even as a child you were always making up stories, imagining things — it's no more than that!"

Estelle sat up, clutching Celestine's heavy black skirts, staring beseechingly into the anxious, wrinkled face close to hers. "It must be more than that, you know it must! How could I imagine Siberian malachite and coromandel lacquer? I know this room well. It brought back good memories . . , and bad ones."

"Of what?"

"I don't know."

She saw the anxiety on her nurse's face change to relief. "Heaven be praised. Who would want to remember?" Again, the same refrain.

Estelle held Celestine by the shoulders and looked into her eyes. "I do," she said. "I do."

Her nurse put her own hands gently over Estelle's. "Then you will have to learn from someone other than me."

Estelle lay down on the bed and closed her eyes. "I know. One must know how to hear, see and keep silent."

The old woman smiled. "*Vrai, ma petite.* But remember also: *I' n'y a pas de rue sans but.*"

"Every road has an ending? That this will all unravel in the end and be resolved?"

"Perhaps." Celestine crossed to close the window Estelle had left open. It was still early spring and there was rain on the wind. Briefly, before she drew the curtains again, Estelle caught a glimpse of a flash of light in the direction of the two small islands.

"I've seen that before, Celestine. What is it?"

Celestine's face was concealed, but her voice was uncertain for a moment. "Who knows? A fisherman, perhaps."

"But it's so regular, like a signal."

"Ah!" The old woman put a finger to her lips as she turned, her voice arch, like an actress assuming a role. "Maybe it's the *faëu boulanger.* Watch it doesn't come to catch you!"

"I remember. You told me when I was a child. It's a spirit, always wandering, looking for peace and never finding it. You told me it could also mean the presence of buried treasure. I remember that, too."

Celestine's face was hidden in the shadows by the window, her mob cap with its narrow muslin border obscuring her expression. "Better to avoid the rolling fire and build up for yourself treasures in heaven."

With that, Celestine busied herself with her last chores of the evening.

When she was gone, Estelle got up slowly off the bed. The dizziness did not return. Instead, she felt stronger and steadier on her feet. The window drew her again, and as she opened it, the night wind rushed in, filling her with a longing to be outside, fighting her way forward against it.

I haven't been outside this house for three months, she thought. But then, I haven't wanted to.

Now the light, or the wind and the scent of the sea that came with it, enticed her. Across the channel, near Jethou, the light came and went again. Estelle was filled with a longing for she knew not what. It made her want to weep as one sometimes weeps in dreams: with an anguish and a sadness so profound that they could not be expressed in words.

Chapter Two

"WE DO NOT THINK IT ADVISABLE for you to go out yet; you are not fully recovered. Think if you fainted in the street."

Her aunt and uncle stared at Estelle across the massive mahogany dining table, their faces registering alarm and disapproval. The four children — two boys and two girls — watched with curiosity between mouthfuls of solid food, a diet chosen by their mama, who came from prosperous peasant stock.

"But surely, if I went out with Celestine?"

"It is too much of a responsibility for her. Saint Peter Port is very steep, built on a cliff. You have forgotten that it's all hills, no easy walking. Celestine's legs are old and she has rheumatism. You are still weak."

Estelle could see the chintz pattern of tante Colinette's well-filled bodice moving up and down in agitation, although her plump little face was placid. Oncle Matthieu's more aristocratic features seemed undisturbed, but his left hand drummed lightly on the table, a gesture he would normally have disapproved of.

"I see. Maybe you are right. I'll leave it a little while longer."

Smiles of relief all round, and an unexpectedly warm welcome for the maid Peronelle when she brought in the *gâche à corinthes,* the Guernsey fruit cake, to complete the meal. Estelle declined their invitation to join them afterward in the salon. They parted with mutual relief and satisfaction at the door that led from the main house into the dower wing.

In the hallway closet of the dower wing Estelle found a cloak of heavy dark-green wool, almost like a blanket, boots, and a walking-stick with a silver handle shaped like the head of a bird. Celestine was in Saint Sampson for the day, visiting her sister. Nevertheless, it was with nervous trepidation that Estelle prepared for her walk.

The air was warm, reflecting off the great stone wall with espaliered fruit trees awaiting the first breath of summer. Chaffinches flew anxiously out of a fig tree as she passed beneath it, and the scent of the first lilac reached her.

With its perfume came the brief vision of another garden: a great fountain cascading, blowing in the wind before a Greek temple, and a different scent on the breeze. Camellias — yes, she remembered camellias. Estelle leaned on the silver-headed cane but the weakness didn't come. This time she felt only wonder and delight. Pulling the hood of the cape forward about her face, she let herself out through the high wooden gate into the world beyond Le Refuge.

Her uncle was right; Saint Peter Port was all steps and hills, and she was in poor condition. As she stopped on Constitution Steps, panting for breath, she decided that the harbor would have to wait. Her legs hurt going down, so heaven knew what it would be like coming up. She decided to go instead toward the cliffs to the south of the harbor where she could look out over the ocean. That way she would be staying roughly on the same level.

She walked in a trance, driven by the goal she had set herself, until the roads changed into lanes. A few carriages passed by and people on foot. They touched their hats or nodded but did not seem to find her appearance strange. A woman walking alone here was obviously not as remarkable as she would be on the mainland — There, she had remembered that, too. How unexpectedly such little things came back! Soon, perhaps, there would be enough pieces to make a picture. "*P'tit a p'tit, l'ouaise fait son nid* — Little by little the bird builds his nest." Had Celestine said that to her recently, or had she remembered it from the more distant past?

The houses were now more scattered, simpler and smaller. They had not the elegant Georgian fronts of Le Refuge and the homes around it but were built solely for shelter and survival, clinging with obstinate tenacity to the hillside. They needed to, for the wind was stronger and colder as the lane led her toward the cliffs above the sea, the cobbles giving way to packed dirt beneath her feet.

Soon there were no more houses. The lane wound between open common land covered with rough grass and the occasional tree that had survived winter's storms, its shape a permanent reminder of the direction of the prevailing winds.

Estelle's cape blew fiercely about her, making her stagger as the heavy fabric whipped her legs. Ahead she could see the cliff edge and a large rock standing alone against the sky. She remembered what it was: one of the great menhirs that stood on the island, once worshipped but still respected and even feared by the local people. Holding its granite face against the elements, impassively regarding Herm and Jethou and the ocean breaking below against the rocks, it marked the high spot on this cliff face from beyond the boundaries of recorded time.

As the murmur of the sea now grew to a roar, Estelle felt the spray against her face and tasted the salt on her lips. A wild elation filled her, the first emotion that was as strong as the panic and fear that come without warning in the lonely watches of the night or during the quiet hours of a day at Le Refuge. Dropping her cane, she held her hands up to the wind-blown spray and laughed out loud as the hood blew back from her hair.

"I am alive! I am not mad! I will remember — I will!"

The man on the other side of the menhir, dangerously close

to the cliff edge, was as startled as the young woman who watched him come slowly round the side of the great rock. His magnificent white hair and beard were blowing wildly in the wind, and his strong torso was silhouetted against the pale horizon.

Bracing himself beside the menhir, he took in the figure before him as the young woman's cloak swirled around her. Defensively she bent forward and picked up the silver-topped cane that lay at her feet, then looked back up into his face. Briefly he closed his eyes as he felt the shock he longed for. "*Eblouissante* — dazzling." Not difficult, perhaps, to dazzle a satyr who had made love to hundreds of women, but this face made him stagger with desire. Then his intellectual curiosity steadied him and he inquired, "What will you remember, *belle femme*?"

"Everything, eventually. Are you the spirit of the menhir?"

He smiled. "This is la Rocque Varou, named for the werewolf — one of those spirits these islanders fear. Do I look like a werewolf, madame?"

"Only the expression, monsieur. You said, '*éblouissante*'."

"You dazzled me for a moment. You must know you are beautiful, madame."

"Am I? The mirrors in my house are all removed or covered. They say it is better I do not see myself for a while, that I might go mad. I have lost my memory, you see. I wasn't anxious to look. I might well have been hideous or scarred."

Why was she telling him all this, she wondered. Surely she should be taking to her heels. But the need to confide in someone was too great, even if it were an apparition from behind la Rocque Varou.

The man was more intrigued now. A beautiful woman, wiped clean as a new slate — what an enigma! She rose to her feet, leaning on the cane for a moment, as if weakened by her disclosure.

"If you are scarred, madame, it is by something inside you or by something concealed in your past." He paused, then added, "Shall I describe what I see?"

"Please do."

They were standing face to face in the small area of calm created by the great menhir between them and the ocean. In a low voice he began, "I see the face of a woman of experience. It gives a disturbing quality to what would be merely prettiness in an untried girl. Your chin is square; the corners where the bone turns toward the ears are very fine. There would be a wealth of sensation in that alone. The mouth intrigues because it has a twist to it and because of your aristocratic curve of nose. Very *hautain,* as we would say in France. The eyes are beautiful, not just because they are that strange dark blue but because they do not quite correspond one with the other as they face the world."

"I squint?" She raised her eyebrows at him quizzically.

"Not at all, no. You are enigmatic, made mysterious by a quirk of biology. I suspect you are also enigmatic because of life's experiences, which you say you do not remember. Your hair is long and blonde. That much you must know."

The woman before him leaned against the menhir, rubbing its rough granite surface with her fingers. "Apart from my hair, I am none the wiser as to how I look. Your description is purely personal."

"As all good descriptions should be in my métier. But, take my advice, madame, and remove the coverings from the mirrors. Risk going mad. *Qui risque tout, gagne tout* — one must sometimes risk everything to gain everything."

Estelle felt the shiver run through her when something of the past reappeared. "You speak French as I do, not of the island." She saw anger in the man's eyes.

"You are right. I am an exile, not of this place."

"Although I am in the home of my ancestors, I suspect I am an exile, too, but why I am not sure. What are your reasons?"

"Political, idealistic, moralistic. Mainly political." He scowled and whacked his stick against the rock, then placed his hand gently against the granite as if to appease the spirit of the place. He shook himself as if to put the past behind him, just as the woman with him was trying to bring it back again. "Were you walking? Let's continue our walk together and you can tell me what little you know about yourself. Where do you live, and with whom?"

"I live at a house called Le Refuge, cared for by my old nurse, Celestine Falla. Alongside live my aunt and uncle and their family. My name is Estelle Gastineau. To my knowledge I have been here three months." What a small parcel of information was hers!

"I don't know your family, but if you are, as I think, one of the sixty families — *les soixante familles* — they will not care to know me."

There was rain now on the wind, as well as the salt spray. Estelle could feel the tiredness in her legs from the unaccustomed exercise.

"Forgive me, but I must return now. I have been a virtual invalid for three months."

Her companion stopped and turned to face her. In that moment, as his eyes met hers again, Estelle felt something that was neither fear nor elation, but that she knew had played an important part in her forgotten life.

"You say you live alongside your relations. Why did you use that word?"

"Because I live in the dower house alongside the main part of Le Refuge."

They had now turned back along the path that led to the lanes into town. Away from the protection of la Rocque Varou, the roar of sea and wind forced them to raise their voices.

"Ask them why you are in the dower wing. The answer might be interesting."

"Why? Surely it's just convenience."

"Perhaps. But there's also another name for a dower wing on this island. They call it the 'widow's third'."

"The '*widow's* third'?"

"Precisely. Ask them, are you there because you are a widow?"

Estelle felt her heart thump, its beat accelerate. "You think I may have been married?"

"Your face tells me so. And then come back to la Rocque Varou one windy afternoon and let me know. There — there's your best way back."

He pointed to the path ahead and turned away from her, moving back in the direction they had come from with surprising speed. Pitching her voice against the wind, Estelle called out after him, "Just a moment, monsieur. Who are you?"

Magnified by the wind, his voice echoed around her.

"Olympio!"

The long vowels reverberated like a clarion call across the sedge and heather.

Chapter Three

RAIN NOW PATTERED STEADILY on the trees in the dower garden. The birds were silent, sheltering against the weather, undisturbed by her presence. No one was watching or waiting for her. Estelle pulled off the sodden cape, now smelling strongly of wet wool, and spread it out over the large carved chair in the hall.

No matter if Celestine found out about her expedition. This would only be the first of many, for she must find out what the island could reveal to her about her lost almost quarter-century. Risk madness, she thought. Look into the mirror and see what happens. She hesitated, then reached out and pulled to one side the heavy curtain that hung over the glass set in the hall-stand. In the dim light of the hall she stared at a face that was at once familiar and yet unknown to her.

Uncanny how accurate the stranger on the cliff had been. He had prepared her for what she saw: the quirk to the mouth, the arrogant curve to the nose, the not-quite-direct stare of the eyes, blond hair darkened around the face by the rain. She smiled at the almost-stranger in the glass.

Like a thunderclap, a piece of the past came back to her. Staring fixedly at the face in the glass, she watched in her mind as the memory unrolled before her.

She was in a coach and four, and there was someone with her. She wasn't sure who, but it seemed to be another woman. Estelle was dressed in white. There was a veil over her face between her and the world, and a bouquet of flowers in her hand. Ahead of her she caught a glimpse of the horses pulling the carriage. They wore flowers and large bunches of China asters all over their harnesses — she *knew* they were China asters.

They were coming to some gates that seemed to lead outside a park to lanes beyond, and there was an evergreen arch and flowers raised over the gates. Then, suddenly, they were passing through a churchyard and the path was carpeted with flowers. It was crowded with people wearing favors like those of the carriage horses, and everyone was cheering. The noise was deafening. Even in the church — yes, they now seemed to be in a church — the crowd was noisy. People were standing on the pews to get a look at her.

She was walking up the aisle — there were velvet hangings all around her — she reached some steps, turned to look at the person who came to stand beside her —

Estelle screamed. She heard her voice rising in the air, was unable to stop until her strength finally gave out. Gasping, fumbling, she reached up and tried to replace the heavy cloth over the carved centerpiece above the mirror. Her back to the glass, she made her way, trembling, toward the stairs at the back of the hall.

When Celestine returned from Saint Sampson, she saw the wet cloak and boots in the hall. The curtain rested where it had fallen, on top of the hall stand. She sighed as she removed her poke-bonnet "scoop" from her head and deposited it on the hall stand. "It had to be. She cannot spend her life not looking at her face, so how could they hope to keep it from her?"

Celestine found Estelle upstairs in the little sewing-room close to her bedroom. She was sitting in a chair by the window gazing at something on the floor in front of her. Only one lamp was lit but she seemed quite composed. As she looked up at her old nurse, the expression in her eyes suggested urgency rather than fear.

"This is mine — see?" She was tracing the initials E.G. made out in brass nails on a leather chest with a domed lid. Brass nails also patterned the sides, glowing richly in the soft oil-light.

"I see, *petite fille*. You looked in the mirror."

"Yes. What is this?"

"It is called *un baheur*. Every young girl has one, here on the island."

"What for?"

"The marriage linen is kept in there, ready, against the day that —"

Celestine faltered and stopped, but Estelle pressed on. "That would explain why mine isn't here. It would have gone with me from the island when I was married, would it not?"

"That much you have guessed yourself, so I will tell you. Yes, you are right."

There was a sigh from the girl. "So, I am married." She bent forward and pulled open the heavy domed lid of the *baheur*. It creaked on its hinges and dropped suddenly back. From its depths she pulled out a long white gown, straight and simple, but with fine embroidery on the high yoke, the hem, and cuffs. In the other hand, she held a small coif and long white knitted stockings. "Why are these left in here?"

The old woman did not answer. Estelle continued, "A nightgown and cap, perhaps? They could be useful — shall I wear them now?" Her hand went up as if to put the cap on her hair.

There was a cry from Celestine, and she hastened toward the chest. "*Nennin,* Estelle! No! It would be unlucky — don't put them on!"

Estelle reached out across the chest and took the other

woman's hand. "Why should I not wear these very ordinary clothes?"

There was resignation in Celestine's voice. "I told your uncle I would tell you nothing, but there can be no harm in saying this. It is your shroud, Estelle, it is your shroud."

"My shroud?" Wonderingly, she held the garments away from her, looking at them for a moment, and then replaced them in the *baheur*.

"So. I know I have been — am — married, and that I am certainly not dead. I seem indeed to be rejoining the land of the living. Why a shroud, Celestine?"

The old woman was angry now, not so much at Estelle, but at the superstition that had made her feel such terror. "It means nothing. Every girl on the island takes one with her to her husband's home. It has always been so."

She hobbled round, lighting lamps, straightening up cushions, hoping the questions would stop. Still the voice persisted.

"But this is not my husband's home. It would appear that it is mine, and is called the 'widow's third.' That being so —" Celestine felt herself held by the shoulders, turned around to face what she didn't want to pursue. "Am I, Celestine? Am I a widow? If so, who was he, this husband of mine? The mirror showed me my wedding-day, but it didn't show me the bridegroom. One of the gentry of the island, Celestine? Tell me who he is — or was."

"Listen." Celestine took the other woman's face in her hands as she had done when Estelle was a child. "I took an oath on the Bible I would tell you nothing you did not discover for yourself, and I'll not break it. I thought it was foolish to conceal what happened to you, but when you came out of the madness, you seemed like a little child. So I thought perhaps they were right. Now you are coming out of that childhood, so I will uncover the mirrors, unlock all the closets and doors. But I'll not break my word."

Estelle knew she was defeated for the time being, that she

would have to piece it together herself. Abruptly she changed the conversation's direction. "I went out this afternoon."

"So I see. Is that what caused all this commotion of marriages and shrouds in *baheurs*?"

"I met a man on the cliffs by la Rocque Varou. French, but not of the island. Olympio, I think he said."

Celestine quivered with indignation. "Ah, that one! Why Jersey couldn't keep him and we should have him, I don't know — him and all his family at Hauteville, and above all that one he have tucked away at La Fallu! Such behavior, and at his age. Olive the cook tells me —" Celestine stopped herself on the verge of revelations better left undiscussed. "Well, the least said the better."

With all the lamps lit, the room seemed much more comforting. Even Celestine's indignation was more agreeable than pity and terror. "He told me he was a political exile — from France, I would think. Who exiled him, and why?"

For a moment, Celestine's face clouded again. "Ah," she said. "Why should it be him, of all people, you have to meet? I cannot talk of what happens over there; I know nothing about it. This island is enough for me. Let them keep their wars and all that nonsense. Let them keep it there."

With that she bent over and started to push the *baheur* back against the wall, grunting as she did so. The conversation was clearly over.

As evening approached the rain stopped, and the air outside Estelle's bedroom window smelled of freshly turned earth, sea-salt, myrtle, and palm. Above the harbor, above Herm and Jethou, stars shone by the thousands. Estelle sang softly to herself:

"A la Grand' Rue
les ételles saont suspendues,
du vin blanc et du vin naër,
nou les mets a bastisaïr,

sus la daos de la tchullier,
la tchullier sé passe,
l'enfant trépasse —"

Stars in the sky, children dying and white wine and red. The song seemed to come to her from childhood, not from the more recent past that had pressed in upon her in the afternoon.

"Had I a child?" she wondered, pressing her fingers to the glass pane and holding them to her lips. They tasted wet and salt, a little of iron, like blood.

Blood. A tremor at the thought, but nothing came. For a child, a death?

Mon tcheur me dit,
ch 'tes-chin, ch 'tes-na,
hors de là!

"My heart tells me, this one, that one, out you go!" Yes, her heart probably would tell her in the end with whom she had shared the marriage bed. The flickering sensation she had felt that afternoon, when she had looked into a stranger's eyes, returned again. It brought no answers but only the certainty of its importance in the forgotten scheme of things, in the shadowy landscape of her past.

By Jethou, a light flickered, darkened, flickered again, and went out.

Chapter Four

THERE WAS A COAT-OF-ARMS carved into the massive fireplace in her uncle's salon. Estelle looked at the coiled serpents, the arrow, and the name "Gastineau" worked into the granite.

"Virtus vitium fugere," she read. "Does virtue flee from vice, or is it the other way round?" Her uncle looked discomfited. Estelle continued, "I would have thought most island mottoes would be in French."

Oncle Matthieu seemed relieved by the shift in the conversation. "Most of them are. We have closer ties than many with the mainland. From there comes the coat-of-arms and the saying. The family is believed to have gone there with the Norman invasion and returned to the island in the sixteenth century."

"So the name would have been 'Gastineau,' and not an English one." Estelle stopped as a thought occurred to her. "But then, my name is not Gastineau any more, is it, since I am married?"

Her uncle's unease had returned. "Celestine tells me you have remembered that much. However, 'Gastineau' is your name by rights, since an island woman usually reverts to her name when she is —" Too late, he realized what he had revealed.

"Widowed? Is that what you were going to say?"

In Matthieu Gastineau's reply was expressed the first anger he had allowed himself to display to his niece. "You must not presume what I am going to say! I do not choose to tell you your married name. You have come far enough fast enough, and there's little you will learn from me, Estelle!"

This direct approach would not advance her, Estelle could see that. Her uncle preferred docility in a woman at the best of times, and this was no time to be aggressive. Estelle cast her glance down. "I am sorry," she said submissively. "I understand, but there is something for which I would like your permission. I would like to see the town and the harbor again. Would it be possible for me to accompany you, *mon oncle,* when you next go in? It is, as you say, such a responsibility for Celestine. I cannot stay behind these walls forever."

Whether it was relief at the sudden changing of the subject to something mundane or because he would be there to keep an eye on her, she didn't know, but Matthieu Gastineau agreed without demur to take her into Saint Peter Port the next day.

The home of Estelle's ancestors, Saint Peter Port, is the capital of Guernsey, second largest island of the Channel Islands, which are the oldest possession of the kings and queens of England. Long before they had ruled England, Queen Victoria's predecessors had ruled them as part of the Duchy of Normandy; the French had tried to win them back ever since. Only nine miles at the widest point, Estelle's island had its own coinage, its own parliament, and its own languages or patois.

Guernseymen live close enough to France to see the coastline but are not French. They give their allegiance to an English sovereign but are not English. Moreover, a Guernseyman is not the same as a man from Jersey or Alderney or Sark, or any of the other islands that make up *les îles Anglo-Normandes,* the Channel Isles.

On the island of Guernsey the Gastineaus were considered of

the gentry, *les messux* — a breed apart in a race that felt itself to be special and different.

"Will these be appropriate for my trip, Celestine?" Estelle had come across a walking habit in one of the upstairs closets: a skirt, tightly fitting jacket, and a tricorne hat with a tiny veil. There was an elegance of cut to them and a lush feel to the claret-colored fabric that did not fit the solid style of Le Refuge.

"Almost too fancy — but then, you're from one of the great families, so why not?"

Whether the townspeople stared because of her outfit, because she was a stranger to them or an object of censure, she didn't know or care. Her mind was on other things as they passed the church with its Reformation architecture and flamboyant traceried windows, the elegant Assembly Rooms, and on to the Esplanade.

The bustle and uproar of the harbor seemed to animate even her uncle. His usually impassive face was cheerful, and there was a spring in his normally measured step. The air, redolent with the scent of seaweed, tar, tobacco, and the unmistakable odor of human sweat, did not repel Estelle. There was a feeling of warmth and security about the streets of Saint Peter Port that she supposed came from her childhood.

Every sort of human being was milling around them: men like her uncle, correct in topcoat and hat, storekeepers and local officials, seamen in navy Guernseys and large shapeless "grigos," or fishermen's coats.

And in the harbor was every kind of ship: schooners, brigs and brigantines, cutters and luggers, the smaller coasters. They moved gently on the water, for the wind was not so strong down below the cliff on which Saint Peter Port was built. Around the inner harbor curved the causeway on which was built the fort Estelle could see from her window. The name came back to her.

"Castle Cornet."

"That's right," said her uncle, the tone of his reply indicating that his mind seemed to be on other things.

As they walked closer to the water's edge, Estelle could see a host of smaller vessels rocking on the light swell. Rowboats darted among the bigger ships like water-boatmen, the little insects she had seen scurrying across the surface of the pond at — there, the name nearly came, and then went again.

Estelle started as the flash of memory returned, and in that moment of heightened awareness she heard a laugh ringing across the waters of the harbor. It sounded true and clear amid the cacophony of different sounds, filled with a *joie de vivre* that made her want to laugh with it. She turned in the direction of the sound.

A small rowboat was coming toward them across the harbor, moving with smoothness and speed. Its single occupant had his back to them and appeared to be shouting in the direction of a russet-sailed cutter anchored a little way out. The cutter was a ship of clean, fast lines, painted black or some other dark color. It carried a great deal of sail and rode high in the water as if its cargo had been unloaded. The man in the rowboat laughed again, and someone on the deck of the cutter raised a hand. Estelle heard her uncle mutter under his breath.

"Léon de Polnay."

"You know the gentleman?"

Oncle Matthieu looked at her, an extraordinary mixture of emotions on his habitually wooden features. They were difficult to read, but Estelle felt sure she could see dismay and apprehension above all else. On hearing her apparently innocuous question, the anxiety disappeared in a flood of disbelief, rapidly followed by an expression of utter relief.

"Yes. I intended to do business with him some time, so — Would you like to go on and visit the market, Estelle? This will not take long."

Estelle, however, was far too interested in seeing the reason for her uncle's amazing reaction. She replied firmly, "No. I'll wait with you, if I may."

As the small boat came closer, Estelle could see that the man in it had immensely powerful shoulders beneath the dark blue jacket he was wearing. His dark hair curled freely and unfashionably onto his shoulders, and the backs of his hands that worked the oars were deeply tanned. As he swung the boat easily around to pull it into one of the iron rings in the side of the harbor wall, he looked up at them.

The trouble such looks must have caused, Estelle thought confusedly. The face bronzed as the hands, the teeth dazzling in contrast, the mouth mobile and expressive. The eyes were amazing — the pale amber eyes of a jungle cat in the face of a human male. The effect was mesmeric, extraordinary.

And, as those extraordinary eyes met hers, Estelle felt her heartbeat accelerate in excitement and recognition. She knew this man. Sometime, somewhere in her shrouded past her body had responded to him with the fire she felt in it now. Whether it had been in fulfillment, as those hands had touched and caressed her, or in anticipation as those eyes had met hers, she could not tell. But she had wanted him. Yes, at some time during those lost years she had felt desire for this Léon de Polnay.

As he looked up at her, where she stood on the quay, she watched the expression of casual interest change. The amber eyes widened, and an exclamation she could not catch escaped him. His glance now turned to her uncle, who put out a hand toward de Polnay as if he urged silence upon him. When he turned back toward her, his eyes still revealed the shock she had given him. Had he, like her, imagined the pleasure of mouth touching mouth, his arms around her as she touched the strongly muscled neck above the fisherman's sweater?

Estelle saw the shock in his eyes change to humor and felt the color come to her face as if he had read her thoughts. His first remark, however, was addressed to her uncle. It was casual, even flippant, and was so at odds with what his expression had at first revealed that Estelle knew the truth was being hidden from her.

"Matthieu Gastineau, you are a man of surprises. Did you bring your beautiful niece with you in the hope I might lower my prices?" He smiled up at them.

Again Estelle felt the tremor that ran through her as his

glance moved over her figure, which suddenly felt ill-concealed in the tight jacket. When he looked again at her face, his expression was puzzled, strangely tender. She felt a strong impulse to throw herself down on the muddy quayside, hold out her arms to him, plead for enlightenment.

"Tell me! What passed between us, Léon de Polnay? What experience have we shared, you and I?"

Beside her, her uncle's voice sounded unmoved, matter-of-fact. If his customary self-control had indeed been jolted, it was now firmly back in place.

"No, de Polnay. Estelle is here for herself, not for me, I assure you."

Léon de Polnay lashed the rowboat to the iron ring and climbed the rungs set in the harbor wall with practised ease. He swung himself over the edge of the quay, and as he stood up Estelle saw that he was a full head taller than her uncle. His sleeves were rolled up, and the arms that had grasped the sea-wall were tanned and heavily muscled. The long legs had uncurled to their full length with the easy movement of powerful thighs. If they had had a meeting of minds in the past, that was not the memory which returned to Estelle at that moment. Hers was a sensual response to this man's powerful physicality.

As he stood there, the wind blew the unfashionably long hair back from his face. Estelle saw a gold earring in one ear. There was a pearl-handled knife tucked into the side of one fisherman's boot. He looked briefly at Matthieu Gastineau and then bowed to Estelle.

"Madame, I am delighted to see you back in the island of your forebears. We —" Here he hesitated, and Estelle felt a wild surge of hope. She saw her uncle's hand move again, heard the change in Léon de Polnay's voice as the tone lightened. "We knew each other as children. Did we not, Matthieu?"

Estelle heard her uncle's stilted response, as her hope died. "The de Polnays and the Gastineaus have always been friends and done business together."

Whatever the secret knowledge was that this man had of her, he would never reveal it while oncle Matthieu was present. It would be better to move away now, to allow them to discuss whatever it was they had to discuss. It would be more prudent of her not to give away to her uncle that her body had disclosed something of what her mind would not reveal. Concealment was the best course for the time being. Carefully controlling her voice and avoiding the disturbing eyes of Léon de Polnay, she turned to her uncle.

"Why don't you discuss your business, and I'll walk through the market for a while."

Her feet felt unsteady beneath her as she walked away. Then, out of nowhere, came another flash of memory: a man's body, naked, close to hers, a sobbing breath, a voice crying out, perspiration on her skin. The impact of the memory made her steps falter on the cobblestones of Les Halles.

Yet it was not this man. There was pain in the realization, knowing it was not his body against hers beyond the wall of memory. What other man? But of course, why should she wonder that? It would be her husband.

"Of course I have known a man," she thought. "I have been in a marriage bed."

As she stood amid the stalls of vegetables, breads, and pies, oblivious to the upraised voices of vendors and shoppers around her, she wondered, "Why is it that when the memory returns, I feel fear . . . and desire? But not grief, as a widow should — or love?"

For a moment, the scene around her seemed less real than the shadows of her lost past that came to her when least expected and then dissolved into mystery.

Only about fifteen minutes after she had left him, she saw her uncle coming toward her through the market. Together they made the few purchases Celestine had requested. Matthieu made no mention of his meeting with Léon de Polnay, and Estelle left it at that. This was no place for revelation. She would dissemble for now, maintain her air of ignorance, wait for the short journey home to see what information she could dislodge.

Once inside the carriage again, she made her first observation casual, remarking on Léon de Polnay's appearance and manner rather than inquiring about his possible role in her past life.

"Léon de Polnay looks to me like the very picture of a smuggler."

Matthieu's reaction was not at all what Estelle had expected. Opposite her in the carriage, her uncle gasped in as uncontrolled a reaction as she had ever heard from him, shock and embarrassment on his face.

"Lower your voice, Estelle! Rumors spread fast on this island. That remark could be taken as an indictment, not merely as idle comment. Moreover, you implicate me as well."

"Forgive me. What does he do?" It was an effort to remain casual at her uncle's lack of composure.

"He is a trader, as was his father before him. He has a very fine, seaworthy vessel, built by Sebire of Hougue à la Pere. He goes far in it — to France for wine, to the New World for rum and sugar, and to Newfoundland for fish."

"Then he might — without fear of scandal, I hope — be called an adventurer?"

"Maybe so." Matthieu Gastineau hesitated, pondering briefly the advisability of what he was about to say, and then committed himself. "Yes, and he comes from a family of adventurers: privateers, they were called. Since the seventeenth century the de Polnays have had letters of marque, that is, licence to operate a ship as a man-of-war. They were great men — great men!" Passion filled Matthieu Gastineau's dignified countenance, and his voice rose with his emotions.

"There is nothing wrong with being a merchant, so why not a privateer? It was a noble profession — patrolling the seas, bringing back bounty to be fairly judged in the courts. My God —" Here, even the ramrod back bent, as he leaned forward toward his niece. "It created a race of superb seamen!

They were the *beau idéal* of all who saw them: active, daring, generous to a fault, and gentlemen into the bargain!"

Estelle listened and watched, fascinated. Was this the same man who sat in the well-appointed salon of his Georgian home, raising an eyebrow when one of his children raised a voice at table? Could this be the same man who had married tante Colinette, with her placid features and the small-minded acquisitiveness of her peasant forebears?

"So Léon de Polnay has become merely a merchantman?"

Matthieu Gastineau had returned to his Le Refuge dimensions. His spine again rested stiffly against the horsehair upholstery of the carriage, and his glance conveyed nothing but circumspection.

"Not 'merely,' but an excellent merchantman. I do business with him, because he is the best."

"Does he ever come to Le Refuge?"

"Sometimes. If you saw him there, that would be why. He would just be visiting me on business."

What a strange way of expressing it, thought Estelle. Is my uncle trying to assure me that all is above suspicion if I see this man in his drawing room?

Matthieu Gastineau's reaction to her apparently casual inquiry was indeed startling. It seemed to suggest he was more afraid of disclosures that would uncover secrets of his own rather than anything that lay in his niece's past.

Although he had nothing to fear from her, she decided there was nothing to be gained from questioning him any further. Somehow she would have to meet Léon de Polnay again, walk into the fire of those amber eyes and brave the truth they held. Would he hold all the answers she was looking for? In her birth and upbringing she might discover something of those other great events of human existence: marriage and death.

The light off Jethou did not blink that night. The air was fresh enough to make the blood race, and there was a new excitement to looking at the harbor, at the ships outlined in the gathering darkness, the first stars beginning to show. Léon de

Polnay's cutter was down there somewhere, as well as the man himself. Where does he live, she wondered. Is he married?

Celestine came into the room, grumbling to herself as she saw Estelle at the window. "Come in and close that, it's cold and damp out there. You're forever hanging out that window."

"Celestine, is Léon de Polnay married?"

From her nurse came the same initial reaction there had been with her uncle. Celestine covered it with a snort, a gasp, a toss of the head.

"*Nennin,* that one! *Il a peur des p'tits souliers.*"

"He's afraid of little shoes? Ah, he doesn't want to hear the patter of little feet."

"*Ouai,* he's afraid of marriage. That's a wild one, not to be tied down by any woman."

"Many must have tried. He's unbelievably handsome, isn't he?"

"The handsomest on the island, some say. But — *'biantai sans bountai ne vaut pas vin evantai'.*"

"That would be, 'Handsome is as handsome does'?"

"Yes. He's been up to some wild things — all the de Polnays have."

"What things, Celestine?"

"Never you mind. No need for you to know or me to tell them. Just look at his pretty face and leave it at that."

Look at his pretty face again. Yes, she would do that. In that pretty face and her body's response to the movement of those strong hands pulling a rope through an iron ring, the swift thrust of his thighs as he stretched himself head and shoulders above her, lay the answer to her hidden past and her uncertain future.

Chapter Five

ESTELLE COULD SEE THE CUTTER from her window. In the early morning sunlight it rode the slight swell of the harbor. A flock of seagulls swooped and screamed around it, wheeling, circling, diving. In contrast Le Refuge was quite still. Only the harbor appeared to be awake. Estelle put on the green cape and boots of her first excursion and let herself out through the garden once more.

On board his ship Léon de Polnay threw the last crumb to the diving gulls and called *"Salut, mes amis!"* He roared with laughter as one bird scored a direct hit on the bald pate of the man he called his first lieutenant.

"Eh, Pierre! Good luck is coming your way! What better omen could there be?"

Pierre Gosselin swore and wiped his head with the cloth he had been using to clean the gun in his lap. "One on your head, de Polnay, that could be better."

"True, but think how much easier it is for you to remove the bird's blessing!"

Still laughing, he looked toward the dock and the laughter changed to a surprised exclamation. "Pierre, look there. It's *la belle Gastineau* — What's she doing? *Mon Dieu,* I think she's taking a boat out to us!"

Pierre Gosselin grinned at his boss. "Renewing old acquaintances, eh? Looks like she's hired le petit Jean to bring her out. Don't worry, I'll disappear. I've work to do below."

With a last look back at the quayside, he gathered up his gun and cleaning materials. At the hatchway, he stopped. "Who'd have thought it, eh? Such crazy things as you hear from France about that one! Seems hard to believe it, when I think of what a goody-two-shoes she was like as a little girl."

Léon de Polnay seemed lost in thought. "Mmm, we'll see, Pierre. And quite soon."

As Pierre Gosselin departed below, a snatch of a ribald island song drifted back up on deck.

Gros papa, gros papa,
Pourchi daonc tu rit autant?
Ah, madame, si j'osais
J'vais d'mandrai a couchier!

"Why do you laugh so much," asked the song. Why indeed had he been so flippant on the dockside yesterday, Léon wondered, when he had seen Estelle Gastineau again?

"Ah, madame, if I dared, I was going to ask you to go to bed with me!" As simple as that, as simple as the song suggested? It had better be; the past had been complicated enough, and he wanted to leave it behind him. Deliberately changing his mood, he laughed and called out after his departing lieutenant, "Bed — that's all you think about, *gros papa*!"

From below came the reply, "Think, yes. We're not all as handsome as *monsieur le diable,* with the ladies ready to fall into our arms!"

Le petit Jean, one of the youngsters who hung around the harbor with his small skiff in the hopes of just such employment as Estelle had given him, brought the rowboat alongside.

"*Wharro,* monsieur de Polnay. A visitor for you!"

"So I see. Madame, can you manage this?" He indicated a rope ladder hanging down the side of the boat and watched the upturned face with interest. The night-blue eyes he remembered so well, in a face that had changed so much, remained steady.

"I shall have to, shan't I?" Without further hesitation, Estelle Gastineau hitched up her skirts and fastened them to a large pin at her belt. She has thought this through, he realized, astonished. Le petit Jean was staring, transfixed, at a pair of slim ankles slowly and steadily ascending the shaky ladder above him.

"*Félicitations!*" A pair of strong brown hands gripped her at the elbow and lifted her over the side of the boat. When she turned and looked at him, he became aware of the feel of her arms in his hands, the softness of the flesh beneath the fabric, the firm curve of the elbow. As if something of the sort had happened to her, too, the young woman gently removed her arms from his grasp, but she didn't look away. She smiled — not a smile he remembered from the girl he had known, but one with a twist to it, a bitterness that spoke of suffering and disillusionment.

"Am I worth the trip?" he asked. Flippancy was one of his most effective tools when dealing with women of the world — or with those who threatened to touch his heart.

"That remains to be seen," was the disconcerting reply. "I have come for information."

He had expected anger, grief, tears — some sort of emotional outburst — but not this cool detachment that he found strangely disappointing. He was surprised at himself. Should he not be glad she did not weep? He gave a small bow and indicated the companionway. "Let's go below, and I'll see if I can give you the information you want."

Léon de Polnay's cabin was a place of austere comfort. As is necessary in the confines of even a cutter of a hundred and nineteen tons, there was a place for everything and only what was required. There was a pillow on the bunk, a patchwork quilt, and a gleaming brass lantern hanging near the door. A ship's chest sat in one corner, the brass bands shining and cared for. An oil painting of the cutter hung over the bunk, and there was a stool fastened to the floor.

Léon indicated the stool to Estelle and sat down on his bunk, leaning on one elbow with indolent grace. His visitor did not seem disconcerted. It was as if her thoughts were elsewhere.

"As I came alongside, I saw the name of your ship. Why is she called the *Nerine*?"

"*Mon Dieu,* and you a Guernsey girl! How could you forget the nerine, our own Guernsey lily?"

Impatiently, the woman pulled at the strings of her cape as if they choked her, leaned forward abruptly toward him, her hands clenched, knuckles white with tension. He remembered how that haughty little curved nose had made her occasional defiance seem more effective than that of any other child. But then, she had been so sweet, so good, so rarely disobedient.

When she spoke again, her voice was shaking. "*M'sieu,* you see before you not a woman in her twenties, whom you knew and played with as a child, but a babe of three months old. I know nothing, I remember nothing — well, nothing that makes any sense to me. What I remember comes to me as if it were a dream."

Léon de Polnay was leaning forward now, his attention caught. "No wonder you could bear to see me again," he muttered. "Your memory has gone, completely? One had heard that you had had a nervous collapse and no recollection of what happened before Matthieu brought you back from France. But the details weren't clear."

"Ah!" She shook with excitement now, and the blue eyes glittered in the dim light of the cabin. "So, I was brought back from France. I thought so, because of the French I spoke and wrote. What was it he brought me back from?"

Léon de Polnay leaned back again. Misunderstanding his gesture, Estelle begged, "Don't refuse me, please. I have to know, for my complete recovery. They will tell me nothing.

Celestine has taken an oath on the Bible and she'll not break it, although I think she'd tell me now, if she could."

"But I'm not refusing you," said Léon slowly. "I truthfully don't know, and no one on the island knows. There were rumors you were part of a wild set in France and England, but we really know nothing. It seemed such an unlikely story about the Estelle we had known. All I know is what happened before you went away."

Estelle Gastineau stood up, and the unfastened cape slipped to the floor. The movement excited him. Her breasts were fuller than he remembered, the curve of her throat more enticing. But then, the little girl he had known would never have stood upright like this, shoulders back, head held high, like the figurehead he was making for the *Nerine.* Eyes down, hands clasped, she had moved like some pious novitiate through island life, the submissive curve of her shoulders hiding her beautiful body from his view. How could he have been so blind?

"Tell me what you know — of my childhood, of the Estelle Gastineau you knew, even if neither of us knows the one who came into existence after I went away."

She sat down again, hands folded together in her lap, as if in prayer. Suddenly she looked like the Estelle he had known all those years ago, when they had both been young, and she had been innocent.

"We were great friends, you and I, best friends. Our families introduced us to each other when you were three and I was seven. When you went to school, I looked after you. You sympathised when I was in trouble, loved to hear my stories. We were both only children, and your mother and father were dead. You liked my mother. She is now dead, too, God rest her soul. You used to visit her in our home, even called her 'maman'."

He stopped and looked at her. Her face showed nothing but intense concentration on what he was saying. "Do you remember any of this?" he asked.

"No. It's like something being read to me from a book."

"Maybe if you saw my home again."

"Perhaps. How was I — What was I like, as a child?"

There was no flirtation, no flippancy in de Polnay's expression now. "You were sweetness itself: very pious, very correct, rarely out of sorts or in trouble." He paused, and then went on, "And that, really, is what damaged our friendship in the end."

"Why was that?" He looked at her, wondering how explicit he should be. "Because I am not pious or good or out of trouble. We were opposites. I may have put *you* on a pedestal, Estelle, but I wasn't like that with other girls. And because I look as I do —" This time the smile was wry, self-deprecating "— other girls were often happy not to be good or pious with me. One became . . . expected a child. You discovered — Of course you had to find out, because her parents insisted I marry her. I would have done so. What else could I have done? But she died."

He looked at the other woman who had been so directly affected by the drama. She showed only polite sympathy. There was no anger, no pain on her face. "I'm sorry. Was it in childbirth? Were you married?"

"No. The virtuous father who had threatened to have me horsewhipped for my sins was driving his wife and daughter home in the family carriage one night. He was very drunk, the horses bolted, and the wife and daughter were killed. He survived."

"*Mon Dieu*, what a monster!"

The recollection had saddened him. No, he hadn't loved the girl — but then, whom had he loved? He had cared for her as much as any of them, and it was a tragic waste of human life.

"Léon." The voice caressed his name, and he looked sharply at her. "Something came to you?"

"A little of the feeling I had for you." Suddenly, they seemed very close in the small cabin, with the *Nerine* rocking gently beneath their feet and the noise of the gulls reaching them faintly through the cabin window.

"I must ask you this," she said. "Did I break with you out of shocked outrage at your behavior, or did I break with you because I loved you?"

She was a stranger to him, and yet he felt he knew her as well as he knew anyone in the world. The women who came into his life now were encouraged to depart before they could complicate his life. His reply was measured, simple.

"I never knew."

"And neither do I."

The reply was as straightforward as his own, but there was pain in her voice, a reflection of what she felt inside. Could she not even recall whether she had loved or hated this man? Oh, she had desired him, that much seemed clear — but had she stopped loving him? Or, had he stopped loving her? Suddenly she wanted to weep, but she did not want to see pity in his eyes. It was information she had sought from him, and she had got what she could. With an effort she asked, "*Nerine* . . . why *Nerine*? You didn't really explain."

Léon de Polnay laughed and repeated, "And you a Guernsey girl! The full name is *Nerine sarniensis*. It grows only here and blooms in September. We have picked it together, you and I."

"Have we?"

He raised his eyebrows and smiled. Too handsome this man, she thought — for my good and his own, from the sound of it. "What does it look like?" The words came out with difficulty, as if Estelle had been climbing the hills of Saint Peter Port.

"It has no perfume, but it blooms scarlet, sprinkled with fairy gold. Ah, but it would be, would it not?"

His voice was seductively gentle, and Estelle felt the tremor from her unknown past return.

"Why would it be, pray tell me?" Her eyes challenged him as they never had in her young maidenhood.

Léon reached out and took her hand, and she did not move. "Because the fairy king gave it to the beautiful Michèle de Garis as a token to leave for her mother, when he carried her off to fairyland."

"Poor mother, wicked fairy king, unwise Michèle de Garis."

"Poor mother, yes. But fortunate fairy king and wise

Michèle de Garis." His hand caressed her wrist. Deliberately, she lowered her eyes to his mouth and felt the response in his fingers. She was playing with fire, and she knew it. She had learned to do this, to get pleasure from it. Had it been with this man or with others? Let us continue this exploration, she thought, and see where it leads.

"What else did we gather, Léon de Polnay, in my lost past — you and I together?"

The reply was ironically serious, as if he had given the matter thought. "Oh, we were great botanists, you and I. Let me see, there was wild asparagus and sand crocus, adder's tongue and yellow vetch, and the wild gladiolus."

Her eyes rose to his face again, and in that moment he pulled her up against him. The sensation that had haunted her from the past now exploded inside her. She gasped with pleasure, closing her eyes. "Did we do this?"

"No, never. You would never let me. Nor this — nor this —" He kissed her mouth, her neck, pulled her down on the bunk with him.

Estelle found nothing inside herself that wanted to stop him, that told her this was wrong. His hand stroked her breasts, started to unfasten the buttons of her bodice. Her own hand caressed his neck, moved under the heavy sweater, felt the dark curls of his hair beneath her fingertips.

There was a sense of fulfillment about touching him. She knew now that she had yearned to do these things long ago, in the days of her innocence. She dug in her nails, heard him grunt with pleasure as his hand began to pull roughly at her skirts.

No instinct protected her. All that came to her was the knowledge that she had dreamed of feeling this man against her, his mouth on hers.

"Take off your skirts, *belle fille.*" His voice was rough with wanting her, maddened by the twisted smile and the immodest eyes that made no attempt to avoid his own. Her hands went immediately to the waistband of her skirt.

There was a gargantuan sneeze from somewhere outside the cabin.

The immodest eyes flared into alarm and shock, as if a sorcerer had suddenly snapped his fingers, bringing her out of a trance. She sat up in an instant. The hands that had caressed him now pushed him away so hard that he was forced back against the bulkhead, banging his head.

"That damn Pierre!"

"I am mad — I must be. What you must think of me!"

Léon could see her fingers as she attempted to fasten her bodice. Bewildered, he answered, "I don't know about you, Estelle, but I am . . . mad with wanting you. Are you just leaving, like this?"

"Of course! Whatever has happened to me has made me insane." Insane perhaps, but whatever it had been had not hardened her to casual encounters.

She stood up and swayed on her feet. Léon de Polnay put out a hand to steady her, but she pushed it away. "No, don't touch me. You seem to have a remarkable power to charm."

Still shaken by the sudden turn of events, he protested, "And you for seduction, Estelle. It was as much you as it was me."

"I know, that's what terrifies me." Her hands were steadier now as she fastened her cape around her. Léon de Polnay felt an intense regret as the body that had almost been his disappeared beneath the cape's green folds. She looked at him agonisedly. "Was I really *une jeune fille bien élevée*? Faultless, well behaved?"

"Completely. Something has changed you."

"Yes."

"Ah, Estelle —" The voice caressed her once more, and she shrank away from him. "No, I promise not to touch you. I'd like to think that whatever it is has set free a feeling you had for me, and that it wouldn't have happened with just anyone."

Her voice rose suddenly and she cried out, "But don't you see, it means that at some time, with someone else, I must have behaved like this, or I couldn't have been as I was with you."

To his amazement, Léon felt an unpleasant stab of jealousy. Hastily he controlled it. What did her past matter? For that matter, what did he care about her? Yes, he would try again to make love to her if he could, but it was her body that concerned him. Not the soul or the heart.

"*Bien,* madame. Don't let me detain you."

"Forgive me, I have behaved abominably." She put out a hand toward him.

Léon moved back, shaking his head. "No, don't touch me. You seem to have a remarkable power to charm."

When her mouth twisted this time, it was with amusement and Léon found himself starting to smile in his turn. "Ah, Estelle Gastineau, I'll have you yet."

She followed his lead, echoing the lighthearted tone of his voice. "Forewarned is forearmed, Léon de Polnay."

"Not always. Feelings like this, as you have discovered, can take you by surprise."

"You may be right." Something had shimmered into consciousness from the recesses of Estelle's memory, and her expression sobered him. This woman was too complicated. Heaven knew what troubles lay around her. She was best left alone.

Le petit Jean had been hovering around the *Nerine,* knowing he would eventually be needed again. He came immediately at the sound of Léon de Polnay's whistle.

From the top of the rope ladder, Estelle surveyed Léon gravely. "I hope that damn Pierre recovers from his cold," she said seriously.

"Yes. Inconvenient, is it not?"

He was smiling as he returned to his cabin. Then, catching sight of his face in the small mirror on the wall, he muttered, "What an idiot I look."

Somewhere in the depths of the *Nerine,* he could hear Pierre Gosselin singing, and the smile changed to an irritated frown. "But for that one and his sneezing, I would have had her and then could set about forgetting."

He kicked the cabin door shut behind him and set off to berate the unsuspecting offender.

Chapter Six

THIS TIME SUNLIGHT FLOODED the cliff face. The wind didn't tear at her skirts but blew them gently around her legs. La Rocque Varou gleamed, the delicate colors of the granite and the lichen on its surface lit by the sunlight. Today it was not a rock that demanded terrible sacrifices. It was a rock to be danced around by young girls dressed in white, with flowers in their hair.

Estelle sat at its foot, leaned back against its warm surface and waited, her eyes closed and her face tilted toward the sun. Far below, the sound of the sea was as gentle and romantic as its own echo in a seashell.

"*Vous êtes revenue.*" A shadow between her and the sun, and he was standing there, close to the cliff edge.

"Yes, I came back."

She told him what there was to tell. He listened intently, staring out to sea. He only spoke when she had finished, and he seemed more interested at first in Léon de Polnay.

"They are extraordinary, these men of the sea! This terrible ocean, it nurtures and forms this people. One is always aware of it, but these men live by its moods and its power." He gazed ahead of him, absorbed in his thoughts. "I, too, watch it every day as I work, bathe in it, absorb its strength."

Abruptly he turned back to her, as if he had suddenly remembered her presence. "The Guernseyman told you little, but I sense from what you say that you learned more from your rendezvous than you told me. When you are on your own in that Widow's Third of yours, allow the emotions he awoke to run through you and see what they bring."

He stood up with an ease of movement that was at odds with his white hair and beard. The stick in his hand seemed more like a sceptre for a monarch than a prop for an aging man.

"Feelings and memories — they are what count, you know. That is why one goes on experiencing everything, both the good and the bad. Otherwise, what will there be in the future to laugh and cry about, madame?"

The satyr's smile returned. "Salut," he said, raised his stick to her, and strode off toward the point to the south.

At the open window of her bedroom, her face toward the harbor, Estelle stood and braced her hands against the frame. She could see the *Nerine*. Then she closed her eyes, felt again the sensation of Léon de Polnay's hands upon her body. Slowly at first, but with increasing power, the memories rushed in.

Chapter Seven

SHE WAS NINETEEN, she was in love, and she was going to be married. At least, she thought she was in love. It was a secure feeling, this feeling she had for Léon de Polnay, whom she had known since she was a little girl. It was like the feeling she had now in the sun-warmed garden of Le Refuge with the high walls around her.

It was easy to feel secure about Léon when other people spoke to her about her marriage and Celestine's words ran through her thoughts.

"I know he's the one your aunt and uncle have always had in mind. *Vrai,* you've not seen him for many months, but he'll be back soon and everything will be arranged."

It was easier to feel the secure feeling when Leon was not there. In her mind's eye he remained the same rather untidy small body with the daredevil smile, who teased her and made her laugh. When she had seen him a few months ago after a fairly long absence at sea, she had been shaken to realize for the first time he was no longer a small boy but a startlingly handsome man whose direct glance disconcerted and dismayed her. She wasn't quite sure why.

Was this response of hers to his looks one of the bad things between men and women that Celestine had warned her about with such emphatic but puzzling vagueness? Certainly, the emotion that had flashed briefly between them had been powerfully bewildering. Celestine said young people who broke the rules and anticipated marriage were thrown into Castle Cornet *en basse fosse*, into the deepest dungeon, and made to live on bread and water for many days. What those rules were was not made clear, however.

In addition to all this were the stories about Léon de Polnay that had got back to her from the few friends she had of her own age. Hesitantly, she had questioned Celestine.

"They tell me he makes eyes at many girls — that he's a one for the ladies, Celestine."

"Ah! Who's been telling you this nonsense! He's so handsome they all throw themselves at him. He has only to give one of his smiles and they imagine all sorts of things, girls like that Carterette and that Jeanne-Marie! His father was the same. But once he was married he settled down and never looked at another woman. You'll see. *I' quient d'la chouque,* that one — He's a chip off the old block."

The shadow over her happiness vanished. Soon she would be married and living with her childhood friend behind another set of walls she knew as well as Le Refuge. It all lay before her, her future with no surprises.

They would be married in the town church and she would have lots of babies. Léon would go out to sail, to fish and to trade, and come faithfully home to her. He would continue to protect her all her life, just as he had when she was little. All that had to be arranged were her *fiançailles,* and other girlfriends would joke with her, laugh, and be envious.

There would be a party, and Léon would give her an engagement ring and a silver tea-service. The de Polnays had plenty of money, so it wouldn't just be silver spoons, as it was for some.

They would be engaged for about two years, during which time Léon would, of course, hold aloof from any form of flirtation. That would be part of his commitment. She never flirted, anyway, so it would be easy for her.

What was not easy was knowing how to deal with Léon himself. His changed attitude toward her confused her, because just before his last departure on the *Nerine* he had tried to kiss her. It had happened within the walls of the garden in which she now walked. As the memory came back, Estelle's feeling of security left her.

She remembered looking up at him and seeing his strong laughing mouth moving toward hers, his lips brushing hers before she had cried out and broken away from him. But what had made her tremble had not been that he had tried to kiss her. It had been her own moment of hesitation before she had stopped him. Celestine and tante Colinette had said that men who tried to kiss girls were worthless, and yet here was Léon doing precisely that. What was more, she had nearly allowed him to do so.

Did that make her wicked? Did that make Léon de Polnay wicked? If it felt so good and so right, could it be wrong?

Estelle stopped herself short at this thought. She knew the answer to that one, for the devil himself made things seem right and pleasing when they were the most wicked. She wondered desperately what difference it made to the things allowed when one was engaged, and what one was allowed once safely married. Celestine implied that there were things permitted but they should be undertaken in a spirit of obligation, not pleasure.

She had once asked Celestine why oncle Matthieu had married tante Colinette. Celestine had replied, "Because she has much property, and it was a good arrangement for both families."

Was this the reason for marriage? Had it played a part in her own?

"Estelle, *ma petite,* come here!" Celestine stood at the French windows, her face flushed with excitement, beckoning to her charge with exaggerated gestures. Estelle knew the moment she had been waiting for had come.

The ensuing scene was exactly as the adults around her had planned it, as Gainsborough might have painted it: garden landscape with family *en fête.* There was their perfect little Estelle coming forward to meet the destiny they had planned for her. Pink and white roses in the basket she held before her, as exquisite as a miniature painted on ivory, untouched by anguish, rumor of war, or the ungodly sexual or intellectual curiosity that can make the best-brought-up children seek to look over the walls that surround them. That, at least, was what her relatives saw.

Celestine laughed and cried and wrung her hands in her apron; tante Colinette smiled in her bovine way and said *"ouai"* from time to time; oncle Matthieu radiated the self-satisfied contentment of the businessman who sees a job well done. Fait accompli.

It was all settled precisely as everybody wanted it. All that remained was to see Léon again, for he, too, was a very happy man, Estelle was told.

Into the candor and innocence of her daydreaming, into the prosaic dreams of sleep, crept a yearning, a warm longing that filled Estelle with wonder as she continued to ponder the significance of the relationship between man and wife. Not man and woman — that would never have occurred to her — but the bond they would acknowledge at their wedding. With my body I thee worship.

The meaning escaped Estelle. In her dreams, Léon de Polnay knelt at her feet, a chevalier before his lady, and she was smiling, pink and white roses in her hands. *Jeune fille en fleur.* Then he would reach out and touch the hem of her gown. She would suddenly wake up as the tremor of his fingers shivered through the fine white muslin.

She made her way happily through the days to Léon's expected return, checking and re-checking the contents of her *baheur*, embroidering and hemming more linen for her collection.

There was only one cloud on the horizon. The envy of her friends was not quite as wholehearted as she might have expected. Given Léon's looks and wealth, it was more than a little puzzling. It became more disturbing when Anne-Marie, a girl who could never watch her tongue, said, "Ooh, Estelle, you're so lucky. All that money, and he's so beautiful into the bargain. Who cares if he cannot resist a pretty face?" And then her friend stared horrorstruck ahead of her, as if helplessly watching the words that had come out of her mouth.

Léon de Polnay returned. It was arranged that the two families would meet in the salon of Le Refuge and then the two young people would be left alone, briefly, in the walled garden.

During the formal interview, Estelle's eyes barely left the ground. When, finally, they were allowed to leave together, she permitted herself a glance up through her eyelashes. His face stunned her. *Dieu*, they were right: tanned skin, dark curling hair, feline eyes. He was indeed a very handsome man.

As she took his arm and heard the satisfied, indulgent "aah" of those around her, she felt the shivers she had experienced in her dreams. This time, she was not shaken by the discovery. She allowed the current of feeling to run through her as she felt the young man's muscular arm against her side, his skin against her fingertips.

They must never, never guess, never know what Léon de Polnay's presence did to her. They might throw her in Castle Cornet, stop him seeing her, stop their marriage. Nothing must prevent this marvelous discovery she had made from reaching fruition. Some day, one day, her dreams were to become reality. She would feel those strong fingers against the muslin nightdress that lay in the marriage-chest, her *baheur*.

They must not guess at her wickedness. At the thought, her arm went rigid and she withdrew abruptly from the contact of his body against her. Together they walked through the French windows into the garden outside.

Beside her, hidden behind the courtly smile and the guarded

expression, the young man's thoughts raced. "Dear God, what have I allowed them to do? This child of whom I was fond, who laughed and danced with me, has turned into a whey-faced creature who shrinks from the touch of my arm! I thought I had a chance with her to be faithful, to 'behave myself,' as they keep asking me. How will I deny my nature if I am greeted in the darkness of the marriage bed by this ice-maiden who withdraws from my touch?"

The tête-à-tête in the garden was brief, formal, and one-sided: questions and small jokes from Léon to ease the atmosphere; stilted, whispered answers from Estelle. The spontaneity of their relationship had evaporated when friend changed into fiancé.

Léon de Polnay left Le Refuge and returned home with his family. He said nothing to them of his misgivings. That night he came back into town and made his way to Le Pollet, to the house of Lisette Belvoisin. Since Belvoisin mère et père were in Saint Pierre du Bois to inspect property there, Léon de Polnay decided to accept the long-standing invitation to inspect their property in Saint Peter Port.

It was even more to his satisfaction than he had expected. Lisette Belvoisin had waited many months for him to take up her offer. Her delight knew no bounds, and the contrast with the appalling afternoon made her seem even more delectable to Léon de Polnay.

For the next two months or so, he walked and talked in the garden of Le Refuge most afternoons with his fiancée. Every possible evening he went to visit Lisette, who would do anything he wanted, for she was sure that was how she could take him from the poker-faced piety of Estelle Gastineau. By the time she discovered she was pregnant, he was sated with her and disgusted with himself. Lisette Belvoisin told her parents.

"No, I would not like to see him, ever again. An apology cannot atone for anything like this, can it?"

Oncle Matthieu, tante Colinette, and Celestine shook their heads in unison, staring at the somber face before them. Estelle stood before the fireplace, her body surprisingly more erect than usual. To their knowledge, she hadn't shed a single tear.

"No," said oncle Matthieu. "You're right, Estelle, but we felt we should convey his request. *En tout cas,* his punishment is terrible. Marriage to the Belvoisin girl — much good will it do them both!"

"Ouai," spat Celestine. "There have been rumors about that one since she turned fourteen. She trapped him."

"No," replied Estelle. "Léon trapped himself. We cannot blame others for what happens to us."

Tante Colinette put her apron to her face and began to sob noisily. "Oh, you're so good, Estelle. It's so terrible for you, the way people are talking!"

Oncle Matthieu threw his wife a look of irritation. "*Tais-toi,* Colinette. Why should Estelle care what people say? Nothing can touch the innocent."

"However," said Estelle slowly, "tante Colinette is right. Their pity is a terrible thing. Oncle Matthieu, you once told me there was a standing invitation from my father's family to visit them. Would this not perhaps be a good thing to do, right now?"

The three adults looked in surprise and perturbation at the cool, withdrawn face across the room. There was a decisive tone in the calm, clear voice they had not heard before. They might not be seeing a phoenix rising from the ashes, but this was a bird of a very different plumage from the timid little thing who had been blown into the heart of the fire.

Oncle Matthieu spoke first. He came over to Estelle and placed his hand on her shoulder.

"You are right, Estelle. You have shown fortitude and common sense in adversity, just as your ancestors have always done. I will take matters in hand and write to your father's family tonight."

Estelle looked up at her uncle and saw the approbation in his eyes. How like him she must have seemed at this moment: cool, calm, all her emotions under control, her dignity intact. Even oncle Matthieu's sharp glance could not see the rage and pain that burned within her at the death of her dreams. She didn't know what that sweet, honeyed emotion had been that had run through her veins at Léon de Polnay's touch. Was it being in love? Was it loving someone to shiver at the fingers that touched her wrist, the glance of those amber eyes?

All she knew, with a certainty that tore at her heart, was that she had been deprived of the fulfillment of discovery, that the pain of losing Léon de Polnay was far greater than she would have thought possible. Estelle was as unlike oncle Matthieu, tante Colinette, and Celestine as anyone could have been, and there was nothing to be gained by revealing to them this secret self. They would undoubtedly have seen it as the work of the devil.

Oncle Matthieu did not let the grass grow under his feet. Arrangements were swiftly made with Estelle's English relatives for a visit of unspecified duration, and Estelle's time was soon taken up by shopping, clothes fittings, and packing. She told herself she was already feeling better and congratulated herself on her strength of mind.

On her last night in Guernsey, she went out after the evening meal into the walled garden, obedient to Celestine's suggestion.

"Go on, take a walk in the fresh air. It will help you sleep, *ma petite,* and set you up for the journey tomorrow."

The scent of the roses she had not picked in many a week filled the night air. The blossom on the espaliered fruit trees had begun to wither and fall, giving promise in their fading of the fruits that would ripen in their place, fruits that she would probably neither see nor taste that year.

Estelle reached the gate in the wall and felt the sadness she thought she had conquered filling her again. The garden brought only painful memories now, not the comfort and security it had once meant to her. She turned to go back to the house.

As she did so, the gate in the wall opened and Léon de Polnay stood there.

"Estelle."

Stunned, she could only say, "That door is always locked. Why is it not locked?"

"Because I have one friend at least on the inside." He came through swiftly and pulled it shut behind him, reaching out and grasping her hand before she had a chance to move away.

The feelings she thought were disappearing surged back at the touch of his hand, clasped hard and fast around her own. Defiantly she responded, "I am not that friend, monsieur." She started to free herself, but he put his arm around her waist, holding her closer against him than he ever had before.

Suddenly she was frightened — of the dark, of this powerful man, at the irresistible movement of her body toward him in spite of herself. As if sensing her fear, he relaxed his grasp, and his voice was gentle when he answered her.

"Estelle, if you will listen to me, I promise I will not hold you against your will. I know how you must hate me touching you after what I have done."

Heaven be praised — he could not see inside her! She put her hand against his chest to push him away, resisting the impulse to knot her fingers in the rough, oiled wool of his Guernsey and pull him toward her once more.

"Very well, monsieur. Tell me why you have come."

Léon de Polnay let go of her. As he stood before her in the scented half-darkness of the garden and she saw the wind blow his dark hair away from his face, she wondered if her pride was enough to sustain her.

"I cannot bear to see this . . . mistake of mine wipe out the years of loving friendship we spent together. I would like to feel before you leave that the memory of those years has a chance of surviving. My mother grieves at the thought of losing you and begs you will visit her again when you come back."

So he was here to plead for his mother! But then, he couldn't have wanted her for himself, or why would he have done what he did? Friendship. No, it couldn't possibly have been friendship that had made her blood race at his touch — even she knew that. Before she could think of a reply, he added, "I felt you shrink from me, Estelle. I think you didn't really want this between us — Oh, I know I sound now as if I am making excuses for my behavior. Nothing can do that, I know, but I have felt from the beginning that your heart wasn't in this arrangement."

Incredulous, she looked up at him. So she had fooled him, too! Léon de Polnay believed the lie she had shown to the rest of the world, because she had been raised to believe that was the way it should be. It was too late now to cry out to him, "Léon, my heart is in this, and my mind, my spirit, and my body — Take me, I am yours!"

Instead, she folded her hands in front of her, bowed her head and said, "Tell your mother I will visit her when I return. As to when that will be, I don't know for the moment."

"And our friendship?"

"That I cannot answer. I imagine you and I will be much changed. We're not children any more, and I'm not sure I believe in friendship between men and women."

Even in the fading light she could see the pain on his face. She was glad — glad she had touched him somehow, even if it were not with love.

He put out his hand but before he could touch her again, Estelle turned and walked back to the house, leaving him looking after her.

He had friends inside, he had said. Not her certainly, nor her aunt or uncle, or Celestine. They would never have countenanced a night-time rendezvous, even with fallen idols. It must have been old Luc who had opened the gate for him. Estelle thought of the motto of her ancestors: *virtus vitium fugere*. She would hold her virtue around her like a cloak, since the walls of Le Refuge had not protected her from harm. She would leave this place of shattered dreams and the constant reminder of betrayal in the pitying faces around her.

She was going to England. Let Léon de Polnay remain in the *basse fosse* he had dug for himself, worse by far than the dungeons of Castle Cornet.

Chapter Eight

IT WAS RAINING WHEN ESTELLE LEFT Saint Peter Port in the steamer for Southampton. Celestine and tante Colinette stood weeping on the pier. The rain dripped off oncle Matthieu's hat and ran down his aquiline nose.

Outside the protection of the harbor, the wind was savage and the crossing terrible. In spite of the protestations of the ship's crew, Estelle sat up on deck, oilskins around her, and watched Guernsey fade into the rain-soaked horizon. Then, and only then, did she weep. No one noticed, for her tears were indistinguishable in the flying spray, and most people were too preoccupied with their own affairs.

At Southampton she was met by her kinsman's coachman with a letter of introduction. Servant though he was, he stared askance at the bedraggled poke-bonnet, the pale face beneath it, the figure still draped in oilskins. He ushered her into the carriage with the peremptory manner of the retainer with the poor relation. In the cold dawn light, in the musty interior of the carriage, Estelle cried again.

She was going to the estate of her paternal uncle, William

Bostock, a widower who lived with his unmarried sister, Dorothea, on the borders of Hampshire and Dorset. Visiting relations and family was an accepted part of upper-class life, so this sudden arrival of a niece from the Channel Islands was accepted with equanimity and without surprise.

William Bostock was rarely surprised. He lived, by his standards, a life of exceptional contentment, divided between the delights of the hunting field and the clearly marked red-letter days on his racing calendar. He attended to the estate when absolutely necessary, relying heavily on his bailiff, and spent most of his time at Bostock Hall in the library. On the shelves around him sat tome upon tome of obsolete theological literature, and in the middle of the room sat William Bostock, blissfully studying racing form and challenging his gouty leg with the glass of port by his side. It would have been virtually impossible for any new arrival to inconvenience him in any way.

His sister, Dorothea, also had a set pattern to her life into which she expected to fit Estelle Gastineau. She expected it, because it never occurred to her that the girl might wish to do anything else. Day after day Dorothea sat in her own little drawing room, working on her "buttony". The hand-embroidered buttons were fashioned according to designs and patterns handed down through the family from time immemorial, from one generation to the next.

In one respect Dorothea had moved with the times. Her favorite relative, Florian d'Aberville, who was a distant relative but frequent visitor, had installed in the hothouses a large aquarium, for which there was a craze. At the same time every afternoon, as if at some silent signal, she would put down the button on which she was working and drift through to stare entranced at her axolotls, fish lizards who swam to and fro in the luminous depths of the great aquarium.

While outside the world moved with upheaval and change through the 1850s, inside Bostock Hall life was much as it had been for the country gentry at the end of the eighteenth century. When in the late afternoon of an English summer, Estelle

Gastineau was dropped quite suddenly into this anachronism of English life, it could not have been to a stranger world than if the carriage doors had opened to reveal the Amazon jungle. On the other hand, so insular was the society Estelle had come from, that she had no idea whatsoever of the eccentricity of the two people who greeted her. She assumed this was how all the English behaved and lived.

"Ah, ah — you came — you are, ah —"

That was the first thing that struck her, their vagueness. Half of her uncle and aunt didn't seem to be present.

"Estelle. Estelle Gastineau."

At this there was a reaction from her Aunt Dorothea. "No. Estelle Bostock."

"In Guernsey, I was called by my mother's maiden name."

"You're here as a Bostock." It was not unkindly said. Dorothea merely made a statement of fact, for that was why Estelle was indeed there.

"I'll leave you to, ah — ah —" said her Uncle William, gesturing at his sister. Then he shuffled off back to the library.

Aunt Dorothea took Estelle to the room prepared for her. It was vast, the furniture standing like islands in an archipelago, scattered at random across the floor. The view of rolling parkland from the window took the breath away.

"Why, it must be as big as the whole of Guernsey," exclaimed Estelle. Actually, it was bigger. "How far away is the sea?"

"Oh, miles and miles. I saw it once," said her aunt. She answered questions after a slight initial pause, for she was unused to the whole business of conversation and the exchange of information. Even at mealtimes, they were separated from each other by several feet of table. It had never occurred to William and Dorothea that they might both sit at one end of it.

There was an incredible sense of isolation at Bostock Hall. They were each an island. Occasionally one sent a message to someone else, and there was a brief excursion, a mild foray. It suited Estelle completely. Her only outing beyond the grounds of the Hall was to church on Sunday, where the parson still wore his boots and spurs beneath his surplice and rushed through the service to get on to more important things. His parishioners seemed to be in complete agreement with his sense of priorities.

Estelle took up buttony and was an apt pupil. She found that the more she concentrated on those little circles, the less her mind tended to move on to other things. It was more difficult at night when the dreams came to disturb her. When that happened and she awoke, longing for she knew not what — for she had told herself it wasn't Léon de Polnay — she would imagine rows of buttons lined up in front of her. Diligently in her dreams she worked away at them.

When a letter came from oncle Matthieu, she prayed it would not mention the things she wanted to forget. She was relieved when she found it contained no details that could upset her, only general remarks worthy of Aunt Dorothea and Uncle William.

Her uncle had a way of starting right off in the middle of a sentence.

"Florian d'Aberville," he said one night at dinner, a propos of nothing.

Estelle looked down the length of the table that lay between them. "Your kinsman," she said. She, too, was learning not to use a sentence when a phrase would do.

"Mm, ha, that's 'im. Damned Frenchie. Bloody frog." Her uncle had the Englishman's deep mistrust of anyone foreign, even the Prince Consort.

There was a snort from Aunt Dorothea. "Florian's English, Willy — you know he is."

"His friend isn't. The one that's comin' with 'im."

"Ah, him. He isn't. Oriana is."

"Oriana is. Just that fella whatsisname."

"Cosimo da Gamba. But he's a prince, don't you know."

It was her uncle's turn to snort. "Pshaw, they're *all* princes, seems to me. Means nothin'."

"That's true," said Aunt Dorothea, with equanimity. She leaned back firmly in her chair, a signal for the servant to remove her plate. "Should tell Estelle." Sometimes, they talked about Estelle as if she were not in the room.

From the collection of incomplete phrases, disjointed clauses and the occasional chauvinistic outburst from her uncle, Estelle gathered they were to be visited by Florian d'Aberville, his wife Oriana, and their close friend, Prince Cosimo da Gamba.

"When?" asked Estelle.

"When?" echoed her uncle. They both looked expectantly at Aunt Dorothea.

"At the weekend. No one travels on Wednesday."

Once Estelle would have asked why. Now she didn't bother. Not only might she not get an answer, but she was fast losing her curiosity. They would come if they were coming, and she did not need to know more than that.

They came. One knew they had arrived before one saw them, for they spoke loudly, in complete sentences, one running straight on from the other, with a richness of vocabulary and voice modulation that fairly tintinnabulated off the walls of Bostock Hall. They laughed, gales of wholehearted, ringing laughter.

All three wore great cloaks. The voluminous folds swirled around them, creating enough draft to flicker the candles in Aunt Dorothea's drawing room, which had to be illuminated early because of the ivy covering the windows. They flew in on colored wings, like exotic butterflies, and found Estelle amid her buttons, startled and speechless.

"What a complexion — what a delightful creature! Why, she's precious!"

Oriana d'Aberville spoke first, in a voice that rang clear and then cracked into a husky timbre that gave a dying fall to the end of her sentences. Under her purple cloak she was wearing a riding habit in a lighter purple, the bodice tight to her body, the full skirt hitched up on one side to reveal elaborately ornamented white lace petticoats and purple satin boots. Long organdy streamers drifted from her broad-brimmed hat. Ahead of her, unseen, clouds of perfume floated toward

Estelle. Black eyes like polished coal pierced the dim light of the room and their gaze fastened on the girl. Oriana's skin was of a dense milk-white color, like the very naked statues by Canova in the conservatory of Bostock Hall — another of Florian's gifts. Perhaps that was why Estelle was suddenly extremely aware of Oriana d'Aberville's femaleness. It was also because the woman now alongside her on the sofa was supremely aware of it herself. Her red-lipped smile fascinated, because she fully intended it should. Oriana stretched a yellow-gloved hand to the man who had followed her into the room. "Isn't she an original creature, Cosi?" she said, rolling her r's.

Prince Cosimo da Gamba was not an unoriginal creature himself. Beneath cape and coat, Estelle glimpsed an embroidered silk waistcoat liberally festooned with gold chains, not all of which supported watches, so presumably were there purely for ornamentation. His canary-yellow trousers were superbly tailored to show off his slim figure and were kept taut by a leather strap under his foot. His blond hair curved smoothly below his ears, and as he raised his hand to push back his canary-yellow cape and smooth his mustache, a diamond cabochon sparked fire in the shadowy room.

"Careful, Oriana, you're frightening her."

The man who spoke was, presumably, Florian d'Aberville, the aquarium- and statue-giver. He was taller and heavier than his companions, clean-shaven but with long sideburns. He was dressed in black, but from the dramatic cut of his double cape and jacket, it seemed more for effect than for sobriety.

More noticeable than even his clothing was the expression on his face, one that Estelle would learn to recognize. It was the look of a man born to privilege, who feels he is superior to most by right and to whom only a few are equal. He was the first one to speak directly to her.

"So, you are Monty's daughter."

"I always said Monty would have made a pretty girl," said Oriana, and the two men laughed.

"Yes, she's very like the Kensington portrait," said Florian d'Aberville. Slowly, his sleepy eyes passed over Estelle. The hooded stare seemed more personal, more probing than anything she had undergone before. She stood up, scattering her handiwork over the floor.

"Oh, my dear girl, please forgive our bad manners. Allow me!"

Cosimo da Gamba went down on his knees before her and started to retrieve buttons and silks, placing them as he did so in the folds of her skirt, as she knelt down with him. As he touched the fabric, Estelle felt a tingling so sharp it made her legs tremble. As if aware of it, Cosimo da Gamba looked up and smiled at her, a smile of such ineffable sweetness and charm that she smiled back, disarmed.

"Thank you, sir, but it was really my clumsiness."

Oriana d'Aberville clasped her hands and exclaimed, "Dear Lord, listen to that accent! It's as fascinating as yours, Cosi!"

"True," said the prince, smiling at Estelle again. This time, there was almost a conspiratorial quality to it and Estelle felt warm toward him, as if he were her ally among this disconcerting triumvirate.

"Miss Bostock, it is we who are clumsy. Allow me to introduce Florian d'Aberville and his wife, Oriana. I am Prince Cosimo da Gamba. Despite my name, I spend very little time in Italy, some time in France, and most of my time in England."

"And, dear Miss Bostock, life would be so boring without him — wouldn't it, Florian?"

"Oh, infinitely so," drawled Oriana's husband. With his abstracted reply and wandering attention, he seemed to have become bored already with the situation. At this point, Uncle William and Aunt Dorothea came into the room and Florian d'Aberville brightened a little.

"Ah, my dear aunt and uncle," he said.

Uncle William seemed unchanged from his normal self, but Aunt Dorothea was as animated as Estelle had ever seen her. There was a flush on her cheeks, and most surprisingly of all, she positively gushed in response.

"Dear Florian, so good to see you. It will be nice for Estelle. She's young. She should have company."

Uncle William looked annoyed. "Don't see why. She's got us and the dogs."

Beside Estelle on the sofa, Oriana looked amused. "Sir William, you always remain so reassuringly yourself."

"Should hope so," was the response. "Now, what are you doin' here? Spot of huntin', what?"

Bemused and bedazzled, but by no means as overwhelmed as she appeared to be, Estelle watched and listened. They were, indeed, down for some hunting. Apparently London was unbelievably boring at the moment.

"Not surprised," said Uncle William. "We'll go to the stables, see Lawson about horses."

Cosimo da Gamba held out his hand toward Estelle. "Will you be riding with us, Miss Bostock?"

"Estelle can stay with me," said Aunt Dorothea.

"No, thank you, Aunt Dorothea," said Estelle. "I would very much like to hunt — if I may, that is. I can ride quite well, I believe."

Everyone was looking in her direction, surprised.

" 'Course," said Uncle William. "You're a Bostock, after all. She's not all foreign, y'know."

Again, conspiratorially, Estelle and Prince Cosimo da Gamba smiled at each other.

It was late evening. The three visitors sat together in the music room. Cosimo da Gamba and Oriana were playing cards. Florian was leaning against the harmonium, idly flicking over the pages of the music propped open on it. He was drunk, but in a dignified and self-contained way. Florian d'Aberville frequently got drunk, as a matter of principle, as befitted his position. Sometimes he chose to be violently drunk, but he kept that for London and occasionally for Paris. He sat down heavily on the piano stool and leaned forward toward the card players, his hands between his thighs.

"Well — well?"

Cosimo leaned back in his chair and pushed his cards away from him. "You win, Oriana. You always win."

She glittered her coal-black eyes at him and started to put the cards together. "I certainly feel triumphant tonight. Is it not a brilliant plan, *mes compagnons*? Is she not perfect?"

Cosimo da Gamba threw up his hands and laughed. "Unbelievably so! A fortune, about which she knows little or nothing. No parents, an uncle miles away on some godforsaken island, and another who sees no further than the end of his hunter's tail!"

"Aunt Dorothea?"

"Leave her to me," said Florian. He rocked on his hands, so that the piano stool creaked, and Oriana put out a warning hand. "And, by God, she has some beauty. One didn't require it, but it is a delightful surprise. That golden hair in disarray — how one would love to feel it beneath one's fingers."

His wife twisted her mobile red mouth at him. "Patience, Florian, we must play our cards carefully."

"What is this? What have we here?" asked Cosimo da Gamba in mock indignation. "Is this not *my* proposed fiancée of whom we are speaking?"

"Of course," said Oriana soothingly. "Your beautiful fair-haired fiancée, your very own country virgin."

Prince da Gamba smiled at her, his charming, sincere smile. "My very own virgin wife," he said.

Their laughter was triumphant but hushed, as if they did not wish the further shadows of the music room to share their secret mirth.

If oncle Matthieu had been listening in those shadows, he would undoubtedly have had to reconsider his belief that nothing can touch the innocent.

Chapter Nine

ENGLAND IN THE 1850s bore the unmistakable imprint of the style of its Queen and, above all, of its Consort, that German gentleman never quite accepted by many Englishmen other than eccentric Uncle William. The English code of proper social behavior was as restricting as the whalebone corsets worn by those Victorian Eves, whom no fruit could tempt.

Notwithstanding, there remained throughout the country pockets of resistance, lingering soupçons of individuality in people who had grown up under the Regency and whose fathers were unashamedly eighteenth century. For some of their offspring, there was a desire to hold on to that old elegance and that raffish, self-indulgent decadence. Such were Florian d'Aberville and his wife, Oriana — an Eve only too easily tempted by any fruit offered by any serpent in the garden of life.

Their friend, Cosimo da Gamba, was part of a European society unaffected by Victorian morality. A young man of confused idealism, he thought he had found his god in a new

Napoleon when a third Bonaparte had taken up the reins of power in France.

By coincidence, it had been in London at a party given by one of the great hostesses of the period that he had met both Napoleon III and Florian d'Aberville. Cosimo had been equally impressed by both men: the Englishman for his ineffable expression of aristocratic ennui and the Frenchman for his air of destiny — wearing in his cravat an imperial eagle in diamonds, with a thunderbolt of rubies in its claws. Both had style, and for Cosimo da Gamba, style was the most important thing in life.

One attachment remained. The other was undergoing a process of change.

Estelle Gastineau fell into the lives of these three friends just as they were casting around for something to do and the funds with which to do it. She appeared fortuitously, out of the blue, staring across Dorothea Bostock's sitting-room at them. The blond hair was in disarray, and the blue eyes above a haughty little nose had a bewildered look. Although her fortune could not have been deduced from her dress, it had already been hinted at by Uncle William in the bustle of the trio's arrival. The incomplete phraseology of her kinsman was explicit enough to whet the appetite of the visitors.

The next few days were a delight to Estelle. In all the sheltered days of her island childhood she had not had companionship such as this. With the arrival of these unexpected guests, Estelle began to realize just how little she knew about the world: about art, music, her own English heritage. There was no longer any need to keep a careful void inside herself as protection against the hurt inflicted by Léon de Polnay. Charmed and enthralled, she found the empty spaces filling up with new ideas, laughter, witty conversation.

Florian d'Aberville talked to her of her family tree, identified relatives in the pictures hanging on the walls of Bostock Hall, spoke of the wonders of Aberville House in Kensington. Oriana was mother, sister, confidante. She showed Estelle innumerable hairstyles, lent her exquisite dresses, took an interest in her stories about Guernsey.

Prince Cosimo da Gamba seemed to be the perfect man. The more Estelle saw of him, the less fault she could find with him. He was witty, an enthralling raconteur and attentive, but never indiscreet in word or behavior. He seemed to anticipate whatever she required. He stayed close to her on the hunting-field, threaded needles for her when she sewed, and played quite beautifully for her on the harpsichord.

It was a time of great happiness. No longer did she keep to her buttony to stop herself from thinking. No longer did she need to wander through the house to the aquarium, to peer into its pellucid depths when she felt homesick for the sea, when the sound of the wind in the great elms outside her bedroom window made her think of the ocean. And Léon de Polnay.

But she didn't think of him often. More and more Cosimo da Gamba dominated her thoughts. Occasionally, at night, she would hear Cosimo's laughter somewhere in the house, and she would feel as she had the night she first met him, when his hand had brushed her lap.

One night after dinner, while Florian and Cosimo drank Uncle William's port and smoked his cigars with him, Oriana was dressing Estelle in the most extraordinary clothing — dressing *à la lionne,* Oriana called it. She had put Estelle in robes of flowing silk in brilliant colors, which seemed to have no shape at all, and had hidden her fair hair under a swath of gold tissue draped into a turban. As Oriana leaned toward Estelle to pin a large ruby onto the front of the headdress, she said, "Cosi will miss you so, Estelle, when he has to leave."

Estelle felt as if her heart had stopped. The wondrous rhythm of her happiness shuddered to a halt. Could it be that life was again going to take from her what she yearned for most?

"Leave? When will he leave?"

"Oh, we all have to leave in a few days' time. There are matters to attend to in London."

Estelle didn't speak, but a tear dropped onto Oriana's sleeve and she started back in alarm.

"What is this, Estelle? Why are you crying? Oh, my dear, can it be that you care for Cosimo?" She held Estelle's face in her hands.

Care for Cosimo? What did that mean? Had she not also cared for another one, now forgotten and far away? Estelle's answer revealed nothing — and everything, for the answer was already in her eyes. "I care for you all."

"Dear child, dear child." Oriana held Estelle to her, and across the young girl's shoulder, she caught sight of her face in the mirror on the salon wall. Oriana saw her own eyes burning back at her with that much-admired quality of hers that her friends called *espièglerie*. The English equivalent of "cunning" is not nearly so charming.

"You should have seen her, Florian! Fresh as Hebe, tears on her cheeks, dressed like a houri in a harem!"

"What are you trying to do to me, Oriana? God knows how you are making Cosi suffer — you lucky man."

Disheveled, drunk, Florian sprawled on the four-poster in the state bedroom and kicked a foot in the direction of the brocade-covered Chippendale chair occupied by Cosimo da Gamba. The prince was swathed in a loose silk wrapper and was warming his bare feet before the fire. He looked up at Oriana.

"Well, is it time? What would you have me do?"

In answer, Oriana pointed to a painting on the wall beside the chair. It depicted the rape of the Sabines, in lush, sensuous tones. Cosimo raised his eyebrows.

"Metaphorically speaking, of course," said Oriana. "She is, I tell you, all yours. Or as much of her as you want to take. Make your ravishment a pretty one, Cosi, as only you can. A ravishment of the mind is what we are after. In the summer-house, in the temple, perhaps?"

"Dedicated," slurred Florian, "to the great god Pan. Cosi conquering among the colonnades!" The parade of consonants stuttered out of him.

Cosimo's smile was as charming and sincere as always. "What a Caesar I will be! *Veni, vidi, vici.*" He stretched his arms above his head and yawned.

Oriana's smile held something more than triumph or

amusement as she looked at Cosimo. "Always remember, *principe mio,* that you do so at *my* pleasure."

Cosimo looked at her and extended his arm toward her gracefully, placatingly.

"Ah, Oriana *mia,* with Florian here, how could I forget?"

In a paradise of hawthorn, laburnum, and rhododendron stood the summerhouse temple of that lascivious god, Pan. In spring, lilies of the valley bloomed around the steps; in summer, honeysuckle filled the air with an erotic fragrance. In the autumn, small wild grapes clung to the walls. The summerhouse was maintained in desultory fashion by the gardeners, since its heyday was long past; Uncle William would only have visited it if horses had been stabled there. Neglect, however, suited it. It was not yet in danger of collapse and seemed to have become part of that nature whose deity it celebrated.

A fine setting it was for a proposal of marriage — for that was what Cosimo da Gamba intended. The triumvirate had indeed conspired at a rape of the mind — or, rather, a seduction of the heart. It wasn't that Cosimo's sexual motives were strictly honorable; they played absolutely no part in the affair.

Cosimo and Estelle strolled to the summerhouse, accompanied by Oriana's King Charles spaniel, Treasure, a lap-dog with what his mistress considered an unnatural passion for the outdoors when they visited the country. Acting as a kind of canine chaperone, he was their excuse for walking together. Since the spaniel spent most of his time in the undergrowth, he was a very poor escort.

Estelle looked shyly sideways at the young man at her side, listened to him speaking of Venice, Florence, London, and Paris in his lightly accented voice with the subtle, seductive lisp. In his deep-blue velvet jacket and tightly fitting black trousers, with his blond hair curling around his face, he looked like a medieval pageboy, a Renaissance Romeo. He smiled his warm, ingenuous smile at her and she responded, entranced, with a smile of her own. Ahead of them, the little dog ran up the steps into the summerhouse. Cosimo and Estelle followed him.

The vines hanging from the pillars blew gently in the wind, creating a carpet of light and shade on the stone floor, its pattern constantly changing. The only furnishings that remained were some wrought-iron chairs and a stone birdbath on an elaborately carved pedestal. With a flourish, Cosimo took off his jacket and placed it on one of the seats for Estelle. He had worn a white silk shirt today, open at the neck.

"No, sir, do not spoil your jacket, please."

"But of course you must rest. I insist." He touched her, and the shock was so great that she was forced to obey him. Hastily she looked down, because she didn't want him to see what she felt reflected in her eyes. It was too late, for he had already seen what he wanted to see. If he had not known it before, he knew now he would succeed. In one swift, subtle movement he threw himself on his knees at her feet.

"Estelle, forgive me for my impropriety, but I must tell you this before you disappear from my life. The past few weeks have brought me greater happiness than I dared hope for, ever. I know I should speak to your guardian and Sir William first, but I must know — Is there any chance for me? I could not bear to lose you without at least speaking to you!"

He touched the hem of her dress, and the young girl's hands clenched the fabric of her skirt. She gave a little cry.

"Prince Cosimo, I'm not sure if I have understood you. What is it you are asking of me?"

He looked up at her and there were tears shining in his eyes, the fair hair falling softly about his face.

"Forgive me. I'm not worthy of you, Estelle. You are so beautiful, so perfect, so pure. I am — I am an earthworm, in love with a star. Estelle, your name means 'star,' did you know that? Estelle, I am asking for your hand in marriage."

Estelle cried out again, but this time her cry was one of joy. He was as perfect as she had dared to hope he was, this young man who knelt at her feet, treating her with respect and adoration. Adored. Yes, she was adored. This one would never touch her, thrill her, and then toss her away for some other light-of-love! Yet even now her response was tentative, born of the uncertainty of an earlier rejection.

"I cannot believe it! Would you play with me, sir? Tell me you are serious!"

Still kneeling, Cosimo took her hands in his and resisted her halfhearted attempt to pull them away. "Completely. I know you cannot give me an answer. I only ask you to give me permission to pursue the matter with Sir William and your guardian. Will you give me that permission, Estelle?"

"Yes." It was said quickly, softly, but he could hear her heart in it. Cosimo got up from his knees and sank gracefully down beside her on the bench, still holding her hands.

"I cannot believe it. You, who are so wonderful — Estelle, my darling, I have done things — I am not . . . I wish, for you, I were perfect!"

"But you are, Cosimo. You are!"

How right she had been to dream of perfection! How could she have lost her belief in true love because of the betrayal of one man? Cosimo's response could not have been more finely tuned to the moment.

"You will make me so, with your love!"

Overcome with emotion, he bent his head to her hands, showering them with kisses.

Estelle looked down on his shining fair hair, felt it against the palms of her hands. It had been the final coup de grace when he had appealed to that inexorable drive in most women to save the opposite sex from themselves.

In appearing to be marginally a sinner, he had won her over more surely than if he had declared himself to be a saint. With his touching admission of imperfection, he had won her complete trust.

"A masterpiece! A veritable *chef-d'oeuvre*! However, I would rather you had quoted from the classics than from one of those decadent Romantics — 'an earthworm in love with a star' — indeed, and to claim it as your own!"

"I thought it very apt myself, and she was unlikely to have heard of Hugo. She might have recognized Racine."

Cosimo lay indolently but elegantly on Oriana's bed, playing with the silk tassel that held back the bed hangings. Oriana, her black hair lying loose on her shoulders, bent toward her mirror, carefully applying egg white to her skin.

"True. I quibble, Cosi dear. You made it worth waiting for in all that tiresome undergrowth. I was only afraid Treasure would reveal all. He found us, you know."

"I saw that out of the corner of my eye, and it nearly put me off my stride for a moment. Then I remembered he doesn't like Florian."

Oriana started to laugh. "No, he doesn't, and I can't think why. After all, there's nothing to be jealous of, is there?"

Her smile gleamed maliciously through the egg white. Cosimo laughed softly, idly tracing the outline of an oriental bird on the Chinese wallpaper with a manicured fingernail. He turned and blew her a kiss, then settled luxuriously back onto the satin pillows.

"Nothing at all, Oriana my darling. Nothing at all."

Chapter Ten

ESTELLE WAS MARRIED in the spring of 1856 to Prince Cosimo da Gamba in Bostock Parish Church and given away by oncle Matthieu, who had come over for the occasion. He had arrived earlier in the winter for the necessary documents to be signed, property to be allotted. Not that there was much allotting to be done. In marriage, Estelle's property became her husband's and Cosimo's remained his own.

What her two uncles had failed to see was that Cosimo's wealth only looked good on paper. Uncle William failed to see it because his vagueness prevented him from seeing a lot of things — although he could have rattled off the field for the Two Thousand Guineas for the past five years. Oncle Matthieu failed to see it because he was so anxious to get back to his island. His English kinsman treated him with the same chauvinistic suspicion he accorded a full-blooded Frenchman, and oncle Matthieu found himself driven into Cosimo's camp. From there, it was a short distance to finding himself on the other "foreigner's" side during negotiations. It was an advantage to the triumvirate they had not foreseen.

The bride was all in white, flowers in her hands. The lace on her gown — point d'Alençon, point d'Angleterre — cost more than £1000 a flounce. Every single person in the area, it seemed, had come to see the fairy-tale marriage of the beautiful heiress to the handsome prince. There were schoolchildren, tenants, the poor of the surrounding villages and hamlets. There were flowers everywhere and an evergreen arch at the gates to Bostock park.

At the wedding breakfast, Estelle cut the wedding-cake to rousing cheers. There were speeches, toasts. Uncle William sounded overcome with emotion. Estelle knew he was just saying "ah — ah," as usual, but she still found it moving. Coffee was served at eight-thirty in the evening, and then the newlyweds were on their way to the coast. They were to stay overnight prior to a honeymoon on the Continent.

Estelle and Cosimo were rarely alone. The other two corners of the triangle weren't there, but there would hardly have been room for them — what with all the servants, the horses, carriages, the cook, and the courier.

The journey across Europe to the Rhine steamer on which they were to spend most of their honeymoon was notable mostly for the poor hotels and their dishonest employees. There was the repeated tedium of formalities on every border. Everything seemed to proceed with the utmost difficulty. Even when they reached the steamer, there was the problem of getting the state carriages on the forward deck and the rumble for the servants behind.

Only an onlooker, however, would have perceived these matters as drawbacks. The Prince and Princess Cosimo da Gamba were perfectly happy. Amid arguing servants, a drunken cook, and broken carriage wheels, they floated across Europe in euphoria, their abstracted manner worthy of Uncle William.

Estelle listened entranced to her beautiful new husband's stories of the European aristocracy, the wonders of Paris and Vienna, Florence and Rome. She hung on his every word when he spoke of the Romantic revival in Europe, his hopes for a united Italy, the glamor of Paris during the Second Empire of Napoleon III — although his feelings about this new monarch seemed confused. A more acute observer might have seen Cosi's politics as being based on fad and fancy rather than true conviction. Estelle just marveled at how much he knew.

At night, after the evening's meal and entertainment in restaurant, hotel, or on board the steamer, he would kiss her hand, wish her beautiful dreams, and depart to his own room.

Estelle da Gamba would lie in bed in the embroidered wedding nightgowns brought over by oncle Matthieu from her *baheur* and wish she knew what it was that was wrong. Never once did Cosi suggest by word or look that anything was other than it should be, on the most perfect of honeymoons.

In the daytime, he kissed her hand, even her lips, encouraged her to buy new dresses and hats, to try new hairstyles. He put new shoes on her feet with his own hands, marveling at her high insteps. He bought her jewelry, extravagant personal gifts. Estelle particularly liked an étui of gold, set with agate and brilliants, a smelling-bottle of rock crystal.

She didn't even mind when he took back the pearl and diamond earrings to settle his card debts with the courier, explaining that "a man of style is always obliged to pay his debts to his personal servants." She wondered though, whether there were debts he didn't pay and to whom these might be.

She was secretly relieved when they set foot on English soil again. Cosimo, too, seemed pleased at their return. Toward the end of the trip he had seemed enervated, nervous. Estelle hesitated to use the word "bored," even in her thoughts. All would be well now, for they would see Oriana and Florian again. A suite of rooms at Aberville House had been set aside for the bridal couple for as long as they might need to find a suitable place of their own.

At the final staging-post before London, they were met by Florian's own coachman, with a phaeton for the happy couple. All the honeymoon paraphernalia was to follow behind. As they came out to meet the phaeton, a young boy jumped off the back with great élan and ran around to hold the horses' heads.

He was almost as smartly dressed as Cosimo, in a tall black hat with a yellow satin band, a cutaway tailcoat and superb leather boots.

On seeing him, Cosimo held out his arms and cried, "Ah, my favorite Tiger! How thoughtful of Florian and Oriana!"

The "tiger" grinned at the prince. "Welcome back, sir," he said. There was something familiar in the tone.

"Tiger?" said Estelle.

"Yes, *cara mia.* Absolutely the correct name for this young man. He's a page-boy — for the outdoors, you know. Other than that, he's quite civilized." Smiling brilliantly at the "tiger", then at his wife, Cosimo opened the phaeton door.

"At last! En route for London and Aberville House!" he cried, and for the first time he put his arm around his wife and hugged her hard, as he gave her a kiss.

From the serene classical proportions of the frontage to the impeccably bewigged footman who received them, Aberville House was all that Cosimo had told Estelle it would be. It took the breath away. Hardly surprising, since the whole was contrived to take the breath away of far more worldly and critical visitors than Estelle.

The black and white diamonds of the entrance hall's marble floor led dizzyingly toward a central staircase carpeted in scarlet, balustraded with gilt wrought-iron. The walls were one continuous painting of Roman centurions engaged in picturesque scenes of carnage. On the ceiling, more allegorically, Aurora the Dawn chased away Diana the Night. At the top of the stairs stood a bronzed winged Mercury, on either side of which stood Florian and Oriana d'Aberville. Cosimo extended his hands toward them.

"My friends. See, we have returned!"

As the d'Abervilles descended the staircase together and Cosimo advanced toward them, Estelle saw them as the triangle they were, sketched on the black and white marble beneath their feet. Over Cosimo's shoulder, she saw Oriana's eyes on her, black as the black marble at her feet.

"Dear Estelle. At last, some congenial female companionship!"

"Congenial indeed." From the top of the staircase, Florian d'Aberville had seen the changes in Estelle da Gamba. Up close, the transformation was even more striking. The blond hair was pulled smoothly back under a broad-brimmed hat with plumes to one side of it. Her lilac bodice jacket was open over a tightly fitting gilet, while the flounced skirt emphasized the tiny waist. The glitter of small hoop earrings drew attention to pretty ears, and pagoda sleeves fell gracefully over elegant white hands. Estelle seemed composed, self-possessed.

"Princess, you have returned a woman of the world."

"Thank you, sir.".

If he had looked more closely, Florian d'Aberville would have seen that the dark-blue eyes were troubled. They were observing the expression in the eyes of the man who looked at her, one she had never seen in the eyes of her husband, and which she had seen before, when Léon de Polnay had looked at her. She knew that there was still something hidden from her, which she had sensed with Léon de Polnay and saw now on the face of this elegant aristocrat. It was something that had not been disclosed by a honeymoon with a husband she thought she had chosen for love.

Estelle suddenly had the feeling of being overwhelmed, swamped in a sea far more threatening than the turbulent waters surrounding her native island.

"If I didn't know you better, Cosi, I would swear that you have . . . had knowledge of her."

"Such delicacy of expression, Florian darling! Well, Cosi — did you?"

Husband and wife looked at the newlywed across the billiard table. Under the low-slung, silk-shaded lights Cosi's face was a picture of candor and good humor.

"You know me better than that! How could you ask such a thing?"

"But you agree she is changed."

"Of course, she is changed. A man of style can tarnish his image so easily. Believe me when I say that the change you see is all done by mirrors."

Cosimo twirled the billiard cue over his shoulder like a parasol, smiling across the table at them like a coquettish woman of the world.

"Cosi, you are irresistible. Such *blague*!"

The d'Abervilles joined his lively, infectious laughter.

The bedroom was fitted out in late Regency style, predominantly in shades of pink and crimson. From where she lay, far from sleep, Estelle could see a superb pair of royal blue Sèvres vases mounted in ormolu and carrying a five-branch candelabra. There were innumerable small chairs in deep rose satin and a scattering of small tables in tortoise-shell. This time, Cosi hadn't even said good night. Oriana told her that he had gone to Crockfords with Florian, that it was "a male celebration, my dear," and that they would be gone all night.

Wide awake, staring into the darkness filled with beautiful and costly things, Estelle mused on the nature of her marriage. It was not so much that she was very happy or very sad. It was more that she was extremely puzzled. She was not so unworldly as not to realize that her assets now belonged to her husband. She was, however, naive enough not to suspect that behind Georgian facades, vases of occhio di paone, and veneers of green Siberian malachite could lurk mountains of debts to tailors, hatters, boot-makers and, worst of all, to exclusive clubs and powerful friends.

Estelle's thoughts did not roam so far afield. They hovered very close to her immediate situation and the conundrum to which she feared she had found the solution. When is a marriage not a marriage? She suspected the answer to be: when it is a marriage in name only.

Chapter Eleven

TAILORS, HATTERS, BOOT-MAKERS. Exclusive clubs and powerful friends. These were the things that rounded out Cosimo da Gamba's days. In between, there were visits to Tattersalls, whitebait dinners at Greenwich or Blackwall, attendance at the Coventry Club, where the rules of racing and boxing were more or less determined by the leading patrons of the race-course and ring.

Not that Cosi entirely neglected Estelle, for he took her for rides in the park and evenings at the opera and theater. When there was nothing else, there were always visitors to Aberville House between eight and twelve each evening. Cosimo da Gamba lived the exhausting, demanding life of the dedicated dandy.

Fitting Estelle into his life was not merely an act of kindness. Her remote, fair beauty complemented his own sparkling blond vivacity, and Cosimo spent happy hours over her toilette as well as his own. He was sweetness itself to her and joyously continued her education. The intelligentsia and aristocracy who flocked around Oriana in the evening were intrigued by the new princess's cool self-possession. What they didn't see was that their fame was unknown to her, because they had not been part of her upbringing in the Channel Islands. She was not overwhelmed by them because she didn't know she was supposed to be. What they took for sophistication was, in fact, ignorance. By the time Estelle had learned about their significance in the world, she had already seen them drunk or flirtatious, losing an argument or their temper.

Estelle never spoke of her marital puzzlement to Oriana. Celestine's answer to even reasonably intimate questions had been, "Young girls shouldn't ask about things like that." Nor had Estelle's contemporaries known more than she. Besides, her immured existence had bred in Estelle a surprising lack of curiosity and a large amount of conformity.

She wasn't shocked by Oriana — a little intimidated, certainly, but not shocked. So profound was her ignorance of what was normal in society, she saw nothing disturbing in Oriana. Besides, Oriana had taken care to see that some of her more extravagant personal peculiarities were hidden from Estelle. As Oriana said to Florian, it was like having a new doll to play with, a companion for Treasure, someone to chatter to and be flattered by. The novelty of Estelle had not yet worn off. It was the happiest winter season the triumvirate had spent in a long time.

With the arrival of spring, a restlessness came over Estelle. For the first time since she had left Guernsey, she felt homesick for the harbor, the walled garden of Le Refuge, and above all, for the sea. London's vast expanse of street upon street seemed far more entrapping than her island's few square miles.

One of the reasons for her unrest was the lengthening absences of Oriana from Aberville House. With Cosimo's busy routine and non-appearance at night, her main companion had been Oriana. Florian d'Aberville intimidated her, and his life seemed as taken up by trivia as Cosimo's. When they were together in the same room, he rarely spoke to her. Often, though, when she turned in his direction, she would find his eyes fixed on her.

One day, when Cosi had taken her for a drive in Regent's Park in his new four-in-hand and she had him to herself for once, she mentioned it to him.

"Cosi, why does Florian stare at me so?"

"*Estella mia,* you're imagining things! Florian doesn't stare at you any more than he stares at Oriana or me."

"I think he does. Is there something wrong with me?"

Cosimo threw his head back, his sleek blond hair blowing in the wind under his velvet hat, and laughed his wonderfully infectious laugh. "Of course not, *cara*! You are perfect, absolutely perfect — still. Perhaps that is what intrigues him."

Estelle felt a flicker of puzzlement. "Perfect? I am not — far from it. Doesn't that make you in the least jealous?"

His laughter was a joyous cascade of sound, and other people passing in their carriages turned to look at the handsome young man. "Darling Estelle, there's no room for jealousy in my life with you. Florian could never make me feel jealous about you. Does Oriana seem upset by his behavior?"

"No, she doesn't."

"*Well*, then!"

He was right. It must be her imagination. How could she have thought of such a thing when Florian and Oriana never showed the slightest trace of unhappiness with each other?

That evening Florian and Cosimo went out together to Crockford's. Oriana prepared herself for a visit to an ailing elderly friend who had appeared on the scene, or just offstage, about a month earlier.

"Perhaps I could accompany you, Oriana — help to entertain her," said Estelle wistfully.

Oriana turned her mask-white triangular face from the mirror and smiled brilliantly in Estelle's direction.

"Dearest child, I couldn't do that to you. It would be wrong of me to expose you to her malady. I must do this, but there's no need for both of us to run risks. I'll be very careful, don't worry." She turned back to her looking-glass and contemplated with apparent satisfaction her pale shoulders rising from her low-cut emerald satin dress. Matching emeralds swung from her ears. It was an ensemble that would have ornamented any Assembly Room let alone a sick-room, thought Estelle.

When Oriana had gone, Estelle felt her aimlessness settle like a lump of unrisen dough in the pit of her stomach. Back in her own dressing-room, she pulled out the buttony work she hadn't once looked at since coming to Aberville House and felt a pang for the reassuringly unpainful emptiness of life at Bostock Hall. Estelle had been prepared for emptiness there. Here, it threatened to bring back the painful past. With a sob of self-pity, Estelle flung herself down on the dressing-room couch and cradled her head in her arms, hiding her face in the shiny satin cushions.

She didn't know how many hours later it was that she awoke with a crick in her neck and the small of her back. Her dress was crumpled and when she looked at her face in the mirror, it had little lines on it from the cushion seams. The candles had gone out, and it didn't look as if her maid had come in to feed the fire or check on her needs.

Her earlier self-pity was instantly converted into anger. Just because Oriana was out, the servants needn't think they could shirk their duties! With a spite born of injured feelings, she marched through the house to Cosimo's sitting-room. The bell-pull there would be answered by a more senior male servant, even at this hour, and her maid would thus be more thoroughly reprimanded than if Estelle took her to task herself.

At least this room looked more inviting. A fire crackled merrily in the grate and the lamps were lit. Estelle walked purposefully over to the mantelpiece and put her hand up to the tasseled bell-pull.

Just before she could ring it, an extraordinary thing happened. The whole interior section of the fireplace started to move. Before her startled eyes, the grate with its flickering flames began to swing through the wall into the adjoining room. Estelle gave a little squeak of fright, which was lost in the sound of the grate turning on its pivot.

It was then she heard voices and the sound of a laugh she knew and treasured. In the space that was left for a minute or so between the grate and the wall, an unbelievable scene was revealed to her, framed like a painting.

In the half-dark, with the flames in the foreground flickering in the draft created by their movement, Estelle saw Oriana sitting on a sofa. She was still in her emerald dress, but her hair was loose, in disarray. The dress itself was now much more than merely low-cut. The bodice lay around her waist, exposing rather flat breasts, with surprisingly dark nipples that looked disconcertingly like another pair of coal-black eyes.

Oriana's head was thrown back against the cushions, her arms open wide. As Estelle watched, she saw Cosimo move into the picture, coming away from the fireplace, which he had presumably turned in the wall on its movable grate. He threw himself at Oriana's feet, and he was laughing. He was fully dressed, but his feet were bare. As Estelle watched, he leaned back on his elbows with his back to the fireplace and slowly placed one foot up under Oriana's skirts. His knee started to move. Estelle heard Oriana's breathing become hoarser through the sound of Cosimo's laughter. Oriana's eyes were turned toward the ceiling, as if she were in a trance.

Suddenly she gave a great cry and a shudder passed through her body. "Cosi!"

There was a click as the grate finally turned on its pivot and shut out the scene in the other room. Estelle fainted.

Up through the years she came, back from the depths of the past. She was slumped in the window frame, her hair wet with sea spray and a light rain. She felt sick, dizzy, cold, but mostly she felt angry.

So, she had felt anger — not grief or even jealousy, really, but anger and betrayal. What had she done about it? Was it this that had caused the loss of memory, her return to the island?

No. Not this. There was more. Piece by piece it came to her — the path leading to the gibbet on which had swung the last of her innocence. The beginning of corruption.

Exhausted, she dragged herself to the bed, wrapped the coverlet around her, and continued on her journey.

Chapter Twelve

ESTELLE HAD FELT sheer, unadulterated anger — if a word that suggests purity can be used for such an emotion. And yet it was purifying in a way, because it purged her of her aimlessness and self-pity.

So, he was unfaithful to her, this husband of hers, who never fulfilled his conjugal duties! Whatever they were was not important, for Estelle knew enough to realize she was living a sham. Almost as if she could see it happening, she felt the anger in her change into another emotion — revenge. Yes, she thought, that would be good. No weeping or crying, but taking revenge.

She thought of the brooding, sultry stare of Florian d'Aberville. He disturbed and frightened her, as Léon de Polnay had, but now was the time to admit to herself that there was something about the turmoil she felt that attracted her. She was not repelled by Florian; she was fascinated by him. He was wonderfully witty. His aristocratic features were enhanced by his habitual air of hauteur and amused disdain, and his elegant clothes emphasized his height, broad chest, and powerful legs that controlled with ease the most difficult hunter in Uncle William's stable. He was not merely acceptable, he was perfect — as was the scheme that now came to her.

She could hit two birds with a single stone. David with his slingshot could not hit truer than she would. She would take Oriana's husband to break her own husband's heart. How he had smiled and smiled and yet had been a villain, this man in whom she had placed absolute trust. But two could play at that game. She, too, would smile and would plan the perfect villainy.

She must, however, be certain that the heavy look she saw in Florian's world-weary eyes meant what she had thought it meant. It would not do to be made a fool for a second time.

Her plan went into effect the very next morning. After a surprisingly good night's sleep, Estelle prepared for the breakfast room with great care. The contrast with Oriana was as complete as she could make it: rosy cheeks, soft hair, a white muslin gown embroidered with rosebuds.

There was a smell of bacon in the air as she made her entrance, which was a little later than usual. Cosimo was already at the table, his hands cradled around a Meissen cup filled with steaming hot chocolate. As Estelle came in, he glanced up and gave her a smile as open and ingenuous as she had always thought he was.

"Good morning, *Estella mia!* How beautiful you look today!"

Cosimo was unconcerned, as loving, fresh, and pink-cheeked as she. Was it possible that she had made a mistake? Behind her, a voice said, "Estelle, my dear —"

The anger came back, and she swung around. Estelle's face was very close to Oriana's, and she caught the shadow of something other than affectionate gaiety before it had time to slide away unseen. No, she had not been mistaken.

"Why, thank you, Oriana. Good morning," she replied, with all her usual sweetness.

It was easy — Heavens, it was so easy! She joined in the conversation, which was about the masked fancy-dress ball to be held at Lady Rowena Saville's a few weeks' hence. Ten minutes later, Florian joined them. As Cosi and Oriana stood chattering together over the chafing-dish at the serving-table, Estelle looked at him across the white linen cloth. His eyes were on her. Curving her lips as deliciously as she could, she smiled, allowing her eyes to hold his for a second or so before the eyelashes dropped over them.

Beneath them, she watched his fingers tighten on the damask napkin he was about to place in his lap. It was enough. She must just tickle this trout, play him very gently so as to catch him with his appetites. Slowly, she placed a small piece of muffin in her mouth, licking a drop of butter from her lips. Across the table from her, Florian's eyes closed briefly, then opened again. When he spoke to her, his voice was as casual as ever.

"What is your costume going to be, Estelle? We know I am to be the Sun King. Oriana is Lucrezia Borgia and Cosi will be Blondel, the Lionheart's beloved troubador. But we don't yet know about you."

"It's a secret, Florian."

Oriana put her arm around Estelle's shoulders as she passed behind her with her plate. "How exciting, Estelle. You can tell me afterward, when these two have left."

"No, Oriana. This is my secret alone."

The triumvirate stared at the girl, surprised. The iron that had entered her soul gave a metallic ring to the soft voice of one whose submissiveness they had taken so much for granted. Her answer was not enough, however, to make them suspicious or to be taken for anything more than a whim. Besides, that this little girl-doll was keeping a secret from them over something as inconsequential as a fancy-dress costume added new spice to their game.

They smiled indulgently at her, amused at their protegée's charming new diversion. That was precisely the nature of a masked ball: to create a diversion for society by which its members could pretend to be other than they were. By assuming a mask or domino, they could live out any fantasy and behave in any manner they chose. Sometimes the costumes and masks were enough to disguise. Even if they were not, the convention was to behave as if they were.

Estelle knew all there was to know about masked balls from her husband, who was an expert on anything that affected a man of style.

"Sometime," he had told her, "I'll take you to a masked ball in Paris. The French know best how to do a 'bal masqué.' When one wears a mask, one always says 'tu,' never 'vous.' One can even express intimacy in the language."

"Even to the king?"

"Yes, my love — even to the king himself."

Intimacy. Estelle had heard Oriana use that word once when speaking about a relationship between a duchess and a member of parliament. "I believe they are quite . . . intimate," Oriana had said, and Florian and Cosi had laughed. It could mean being good friends, but Estelle was sure that was not what was meant in this case. Florian and Cosi and Oriana were all intimates, were they not? Oriana and Cosi certainly appeared to be. She, however, was intimate with no one, not even her own husband.

In her empty hours, Estelle had discovered Florian's library. It was very different from Uncle William's, and she had found herself surrounded by the likes of Swift, Shakespeare, Bossuet, and Voltaire. And, while browsing among them, she had discovered Florian's books on art.

These books shocked and fascinated her. The women painted by the Dutch masters were recognizable as the good bourgeoises of her island, but there was an array of female beauty immortalized in activities and states of undress that quite amazed her. In the middle range between propriety and licentiousness, one in particular had stayed in her mind. The painting by François Boucher was of Madame de Pompadour, Louis XV's favorite mistress; it was the wrong Louis, but no matter. The allusion was right, and besides, Estelle admired the dress. Armed with Florian's art book, she set off to her dress-maker.

Everyone was only too happy to indulge her with her secret. They had agreed to meet in the library on the night of the ball and to toast each other's costumes in front of the great Tudor fireplace, beneath the domed ceiling. They had chosen the library, because they could all arrive by different doors at the same time and make a grand entrance.

Fifteen minutes before the appointed time, Estelle placed herself on the Regency sofa at the end of the room, where she would be visible from all three doors. Carefully she imitated the Boucher pose: skirt spread over the sofa, one hand on the cushions, another holding a book on her lap. Even Treasure obliged by sitting at her feet like the marquise's little dog in the painting. Calmly, she waited.

Precisely on time, three doors opened. Louis XIV, Lucrezia Borgia, and Blondel found themselves gazing at Madame de Pompadour.

She was dressed in dark green shot-silk, with an enormous panniered and flounced skirt decorated with pale and burnt-orange roses, the sleeves edged with gold lace and large orange bows. The bodice was cut tight and extremely low, and it was composed entirely of burnt-orange bows. Around her slim neck was a bright orange organdy ruffle, and her blond hair was pulled back from her face and held by tiny orange flowers. Beneath the skirt her feet showed in tiny orange satin shoes with high heels.

It was the marquise herself looking calmly back at them, a slight smile curving her lips. No quiet Dresden maid this, but a woman of the world showing her true colors. Florian spoke first.

"Estelle, you are magnificent. You have outdone us all."

Oriana, in black velvet and diamonds, was patently angry. Cosimo, in white satin, blond hair in medieval pageboy style, held his mandolin down to his side and looked petulant, disconcerted. It was only the games in life that he took seriously, and he had been outmaneuvered on this one.

"You broke the rules, Estelle. That's not fair of you."

"Of course, she did. But she would have upstaged us,

anyway. Let us applaud her." Florian was smiling, as if at some secret joke. Beneath the plumes of his hat, his expression was quizzical, speculative.

With a visible effort, Oriana pulled herself together and laughed. "Bravo, Estelle darling. No wonder you wanted to keep your secret. What a clever girl you are."

Lightheartedly, Cosimo advanced toward her, arms outstretched. "My beautiful wife. How proud I am of you! How well you complement me!"

Behind him, Florian said, "I think it's more that you complement her, Cosi, dear boy. You look like an attendant to a great princess."

Estelle felt actual pleasure when she saw the anger in Cosi's eyes, watched his lips quiver. He swung around and said to Florian, "In that case, perhaps you as a king are the one who should escort my wife. I will go with your wife."

She couldn't have written more advantageous dialogue herself. Estelle looked to see if Florian were showing anger or jealousy. He seemed the same as ever, bored but amused.

"Of course, dear chap, delighted. Anything to oblige a friend."

Abruptly, Cosimo turned on his heel and left the room, extending his arm for Oriana as he passed her. Lazily, Florian put up a hand and waved good-bye. The door closed and they were on their own.

"I'm sorry, Florian. I didn't mean that to happen."

"Yes, you did." Florian was laughing, something which he did far less than Oriana or Cosi. "Have you been using my library?"

"Yes. Do you mind?"

"No. Did you by any chance read Molière while you were there?"

"Some, yes. Why?"

"This reminds me of his play, *The School for Wives*. Take 'em young, make of them what you want. Didn't work there, either."

Estelle raised her eyebrows. "What have I done wrong?"

"I suspect you have picked up more than we intended far too quickly, that's all." Florian knelt in front of her, then picked up her hand and kissed it. There was no other attempt at the intimacy she had hoped to bring about.

"Come, Madame la Marquise, let's make our grand entrance at the Savilles' ball."

He helped her to her feet and looked quite serious for a moment. "You have proved to be unpredictable, Estelle. I have rarely felt less bored in my life."

"What a beautifully understated compliment, sir."

This time he laughed outright. "How we have underestimated you! You're far brighter than we thought."

"I am far brighter than I thought I was, so you mustn't blame yourselves, Florian."

This time, she joined in his laughter, felt her heartbeat accelerate at his amused gaze, at her own daring, at the dangerous game she was playing.

Chapter Thirteen

HIDDEN BEHIND HER ORANGE SILK MASK, Estelle was one of the few people that night who went genuinely unrecognized. The small slip of silk over her eyes gave her a courage far out of proportion to its size and the amount of her that it concealed. Amid some of the most brilliant and beautiful people in London, Estelle felt articulate, witty, safe, as protected as she had been behind the walls of Le Refuge.

What was more, the men with whom she talked and danced treated her as the woman she portrayed. They showed a fascinated deference and a salacious suggestiveness that lay beyond her realm of experience. It didn't matter. Estelle found that these men responded to the elusive reply, the knowing smile, quite as satisfactorily as to anything more precise. They presumed she knew and understood their remarks. She had become for them the costume she wore, and when she saw herself in the long mirrors around the ballroom, she began to believe it herself. Fascinated, she watched herself flirt and laugh with the men who surrounded her.

Once Oriana was assured that her black-and-silver Borgia costume had achieved the desired effect, she recovered her equilibrium. She spent a considerable amount of time dancing with their host, Lord Saville, whose shock of red hair under his Viking helmet made him easily recognizable. Cosimo seemed unperturbed by this and divided his time between a group of gambling cronies, including Florian, and Estelle. He now seemed enchanted with his wife's success and anxious that she should be seen as his.

His new-found delight in her changed what she had expected to happen at the end of the evening. She found herself in her husband's cabriolet, going back to Aberville House with a still-effervescent and chattering Cosi beside her. Florian and Oriana were nowhere to be seen.

Listening to the tender words he had for her, Estelle wondered if things had perhaps changed between them. His arm around her, he picked up her hand and held it to his lips. "*Estella mia,*" he sighed.

On the floor of the carriage, his white satin-clad foot tapped out a rhythm and she saw again the scene framed by the fireplace. How ironic it would be if he wanted her, now that all she felt was anger!

She needn't have worried. At Aberville House, he kissed her tenderly at the door of her bedroom and left her, walking jauntily off down the long corridor. She was still alone.

Tears came to her this time. Without her mask, she was still just Estelle da Gamba dressed as Madame de Pompadour — a poor, frightened thing, manipulated by those she had trusted. With shaking fingers, she took the mask from her *étui* and put it on again.

Better. That was better. Behind the mask, the tears gave her eyes a superficial glitter almost like Oriana's. She unfastened the bodice and overskirt of her dress and let them drop to the floor. With her mask, the orange ruffle still around her neck, she felt protected against the world. The tight basque she was wearing pushed her breasts high, made the tiny waist even smaller. She smiled at her reflection.

"You are magnificent, Estelle."

Her heartbeat felt as if it would burst the tight bodice. She cried out. "Who *dares* to —"

"I do." Florian d'Aberville was sitting on her bed, concealed by the curtains, which he now pushed to one side. He was wearing only the hose and the silk shirt of his costume, which was open to the waist. He looked as she had seen him look when not yet quite drunk, when the wine had given him an air of restlessness, as if he would break out of the aura of boredom that surrounded him. At such moments, he seemed unpredictable, even dangerous — all the more dangerous now she knew she was attracted by those qualities.

"Florian — I'm getting ready for bed — I'm undressing." How swiftly that articulate sophistication had deserted her! What more ill-advised remark could she have found to say, she thought despairingly.

"I am well aware of that." He got up off the bed and was moving toward her with a sureness that showed he was certainly not hopelessly drunk.

"What are you doing here, Florian?" she asked fearfully.

"You know what I am doing here."

Yes, she did . . . and no, she didn't. This was what she wanted, wasn't it? Utterly confused, she felt the tears trickle under the silk mask. His hands were on her shoulders now, stroking her throat and her nearly exposed breasts.

"I must tell you, Estelle, I intend to have you. You have played me for a while and here I am, as you planned."

"Florian, I planned nothing! I only wanted to flirt with you, to make them jealous! Because of what I saw!"

"Ah, you saw something. Hence the pretty smiles, the flirtatious glances. Making them jealous, eh? Let's see what we can do."

He had pulled her against him now, holding her tightly around the waist, forcing her head back with the urgency of his kisses. She felt her legs part, his hands start to pull at her skirt, ripping the flimsy fabric from her. She started to struggle. All she felt now was fear.

"No, Estelle, don't fight me — I promise you we will make them jealous. I'll do all I can to satisfy your wishes — and mine." Still holding her around the waist, he ripped off the basque so that the laces broke and threw it away onto the floor. Desperately, she tried to hold him off, pushing against his chest, pleading with him.

"No, no — this is wrong, wicked — this is for marriage — let me go, please let me go!"

Almost naked now, held against him by one arm, she saw that he had started to rip away his own garments, pushing her toward the bed.

"Marriage? This is for marriage? But you don't do this with Cosi, do you, so what does it matter? Look at you — wasted on Cosi! I only do what he will never do to you."

"Yes, he has! You're wrong, he has!"

"No — he — hasn't."

Estelle made one last lunge at him, going for his face as he caught her up and took her to the bed. She was appalled now by his strength, terrified by whatever was about to happen, of the unknown she thought she had wanted to discover. "I — don't — want — this!"

"Yes, you do, yes you do, yes you do." He said it again and again as he took her, holding her arms, the weight of his body pinning her beneath him.

She thought she was going to die. She knew she was going to die. She heard herself call out, as if it were another woman's voice. "No, I don't!"

And in that moment she felt the resistance go out of her body. It was not from submission to the inevitable but from the sudden rush of pleasure that hit her uncontrollably. She felt his thighs move against hers, the silk of the shirt he still wore brush her breasts, the pressure of him within her, releasing emotions her upbringing had refused to acknowledge and made her deny.

Denial was pointless any more. In spite of herself she was responding to this man's violation, and as she felt the driving rhythm of his body against hers she echoed it instinctively, hearing the gasp of her breath as it caught in her throat. Suddenly, she was engulfed by a wave of feeling that hit her with a force as devastating as that of the great seas off Jethou.

Disoriented, exhausted, she sat up on the bed and put her shaking hands to her face. She realized she was still wearing the orange silk mask and organdy ruffle. She saw a garden, pink and white roses, Estelle, *jeune fille en fleur*. Tears came into the eyes again.

What had happened seemed all the more terrible, because of her feelings that had been released. She looked at the man lying beside her, at the elegant strength of his wide shoulders and tapering waist, the seduction of those lazy, sleepy eyes.

"*En basse fosse*. We shall be thrown into *le basse fosse*."

She must have spoken the words out loud, for Florian replied, "No dungeons, Estelle. You have just been set free from a dungeon."

"Wicked, cruel."

"Yes, I hadn't intended it that way. I didn't think you would fight me."

"I didn't want it. I told you I didn't want it."

"Yes, you did."

Yes, yes she had. Not quite like that, but she had. "Leave me alone."

"Not now. It becomes more of a violation if I leave you now."

Estelle was too tired to argue. She removed the ruffle and the mask and dropped them on the floor. Then she turned over on her side and went to sleep.

Florian was still with her when she awoke. Foggily, her thoughts groped toward what had happened. She turned over on the bed and looked at her ravisher.

He was sound asleep, his hand curled under his cheek like a small child, the coverlet caught about his legs. Estelle sat up and looked at him. When she regarded the powerful body that had overwhelmed her, she was most aware of the utter vulnerability of a human being asleep.

"I could kill him. I could put my Spanish paper-knife through his heart. It's sharp enough."

Why should she kill him? Was this not what Léon de Polnay had wanted of her? It was too late now for such thoughts. They should be put behind her in the past with the ignorance that had lost her one man and made her victim to another. No, not Florian, but Cosimo da Gamba, her husband. She no longer felt the victim of the man who lay beside her, achingly vulnerable in his sleep.

Florian d'Aberville moved slightly and a smile flickered across his lips. Instinctively, Estelle put out her hand and pulled the coverlet up around his shoulders. He was stronger than she was, more powerful in society and her seducer, but she sensed in him an insecurity greater than her own. Like countless women before her or since, Estelle felt the tug of an instinct as compelling as the lust — or love — that had possessed them both only a few hours before.

Chapter Fourteen

WHEN FLORIAN AWOKE, he put out his hand and traced the line of her jaw, the curve of her shoulder, gently, almost timidly.

"Rose petals floating in milk, just like Boucher's women. Estelle, the star-lady."

She didn't realize it, but Estelle was watching her seducer fall in love with her. He alone knew it and knew how it made him tremble. Florian moved slowly this time, terrified she would run away, knowing he could never take her by force again, a violator caught by his own act of violence.

"Don't leave, Estelle. I won't touch you again unless you want it."

She smiled, a sad half-smile. "I can't, really. This is my bedroom."

He caught her hand and kissed it. "Don't leave this house, this country, return to your island."

Estelle stirred a little, but left her hand where it was. "I can't do that. It would spoil my plan." She pulled the sheet across her body, as carefully as a few moments earlier she had covered him. With a gesture much like her own, the gesture he hadn't seen, Florian smoothed the sheet around her shoulders.

"Now, tell me your plan."

"To make Cosimo and Oriana jealous — to see them suffer for what they have done to me."

She saw concern on his face and realized she might hurt him, too. "They — they have done what you and I did — have just done together."

Instantly, the concern changed to what looked incredibly like amusement. "Estelle, my dear, it's not possible. You'll have to tell me what you saw, because it has to have been something else. And how, in God's name, did you see anything?"

"Through the fireplace in Cosi's room that turns."

"Ah, you saw through into Oriana's day-room. What were they doing?"

Haltingly, stumbling over her words, she told him. When she had finished, there was complete silence. She had averted her eyes as she relived the scene, and when she looked at him, his expression again surprised her, for it looked very much like pity. She felt she had seen more changes on Florian's aristocratic features in the last five minutes than in all the previous months she had known him.

"Are you just sorry for me, Florian? Don't you feel anger for yourself?"

He gave a sigh, and it was a while before he answered her. "No point in not coming out with it. I took some of your innocence tonight, and now I must take some more. No, I don't feel angry. Estelle, my dear, your husband will never make love to you and has never made love to Oriana — not as you and I made love, that is. He is not interested in women, and we can leave it at that. However, he does find it extremely amusing to . . . perform certain services for Oriana in the way that you saw that night. I suspect it is one of their favorite pastimes. He stimulates her while she tells him in precise detail of her latest amorous assignation, until she relives in his presence the moment of climax. They both adore that."

Horrified, she reverted to a child's method of shutting out what it doesn't want to see. She put her hands over her face, but the gesture didn't stop the images that danced in her mind's eye.

"That is — that is *grotesque*!"

"A good word for it. Would it make it any better if I said I have not found such grotesqueries amusing for many months? That I haven't partaken of such amusements since you came on the scene?"

The dark-blue eyes stared at him over the top of her hands, and then the words burst out of her. "Make it any better? I don't know if I can believe you, do I? And it alters nothing about Oriana and Cosi, does it? Does it?"

Suddenly she leaned forward and grabbed his shoulders in anger, the sheet around her own shoulders forgotten. When he closed his eyes as she spoke, it was not the words that affected him, but the beauty of the young woman's body revealed again to him.

"They are your wife and your friend, Florian — your wife and your friend. And you live with them? You *like* them?"

He opened his eyes and looked straight at her. His features were impassive again, but somehow she was aware of a great wave of pain that washed between them. Then, with a twitch of the mouth, he returned to the withdrawn hauteur, the bored voice of the man she had first known at Bostock Hall.

"Incredible, isn't it, Estelle — the most outrageous thing of all these outrageous things. Yes, I do. I like them. They are my friends."

She took her hands away and held the sheet against her again, shaking her head in disbelief.

"I knew nothing, did I? I knew even less than I thought I knew. It was only for my money, wasn't it? For the three of you."

Toneless, expressionless, he repeated what she had said. "It was for your money, for the three of us."

As she started to weep, he put out his arms and drew her

against him. She had no one else to comfort her so she let him hold her.

After a while, he put up a hand and started to stroke her hair. Then he said, "You have one small victory, Estelle."

She was crying no longer, but he felt her tremble against him and was shaken by the mixture of longing and compassion that assailed him. He held her away from him and put his hands on each side of her tear-swollen face. "You have me, Estelle. For what it's worth, you have me."

She smiled slightly, but all she said was, "I'm tired now. I'm going to sleep again."

When she woke the room was light and Florian had gone. She recognized the fact with an unexpected feeling of deprivation and a growing sense of unreality.

It was late afternoon when Estelle came out of her room. She asked her personal maid where everyone was.

"I don't know where Prince Cosimo and Lady Oriana are, your highness, but Lord d'Aberville is in the library."

Florian was sitting on the sofa on which he had first seen her as Madame de Pompadour, and appeared to be writing a letter. His expression and attitude seemed as languid as ever, but when he looked up at her, Estelle was struck by the look in his eyes. It was like Treasure's expression when he was longing for a walk.

"Good afternoon, Florian. Where are the others?"

When he spoke, Florian's voice did not match the look in his eyes. It was as drawling and unconcerned as ever. "Sit down, Estelle. We must talk — no, not about what you might imagine, but about Oriana and Cosimo."

"Where are they?" Estelle repeated.

Florian swung his legs down off the sofa and leaned toward her. "This morning while you slept they left for France. Their departure was sudden, I know, but it has nothing to do with what I have no doubt you are imagining. It has to do with politics, kings, and power."

He put out a hand as if he would touch her and then stopped.

"We weren't going to tell you very much about this, but things have changed since last night. At least, my position has changed. I'm supposed to be with them."

Bewildered, Estelle asked, "You mean that the three of you were simply going to leave me?"

"Yes. Their departure wasn't planned — the news came suddenly. I won't pretend we didn't expect it for some time, but we hadn't planned to leave this morning. And there's no point in pretending we hadn't already decided to leave you once the news did come." This time he did touch her, holding her as she got up out of the chair opposite him, forcing her to sit down again.

"Don't you see the amusing side, Estelle? I changed everything for myself when I made love to you last night, against your will. Here I sit, with a very angry young woman, who is quite likely to run that poker through me when I let go of her, instead of carousing with my good friends at the court of Napoleon III."

He felt the tension go out of her, and slowly he let her go.

"I thought of killing you last night," she said.

"Ah, Estelle, I'm not worth it. A lifetime in prison — or worse — for the likes of me? Sit for a while and let me explain what I would never have dreamt of telling you a mere twenty-four hours ago."

His eyes fixed on the fire, he started to talk. "I met Cosimo a few years ago on his first visit to London, at Lady Holland's. Also present on that occasion was the man who is now Napoleon III and was then in exile here."

"Exile *here*," said Estelle, puzzled. "I wouldn't have thought a Napoleon would have set foot on English soil."

"Ah," said Florian. "But this Napoleon is not the famous Bonaparte, although his name still dazzles people like our Cosi. This one is a nephew of that great Bonaparte, and our nation and France have changed their allegiances since then. Besides, all royalty tends to stick together, you know. Better a crowned head of dubious lineage, like this Louis Napoleon, than a French republic." Florian smiled reminiscently.

"Even I have to admit he made one very aware of his sense of destiny, his determination to lead France out of what he saw as a wilderness. I had little to do with him, but Cosi became enamored of his air of mystery and, above all, of his name: Napoleon. Of course, half of Cosi's family is French and much of his education was in Paris, so it's hardly surprising. He was elated when Napoleon took power and then became Emperor and married Eugénie. His court has style, panache, romanticism — all the things Cosi adores." Florian now turned away from the fire and his expression changed, as if this part of the story did not give him as much pleasure.

"Since then, many things have changed. Napoleon is not really liberal, and he's not very much interested in the arts. Much of the style is Eugénie's, not his. The games that really absorb him are those of power politics. And for all Cosi's protestations, he is interested in the form, not the content. He's become bored with Napoleon, disillusioned now the mystery has gone."

"Then why has he gone off to France?" asked Estelle.

Florian smiled at her. "Because another man of destiny has come along. What's more, he's Italian. It is this man that Cosi and Oriana have gone to meet."

He looked as if he would stop at his point, but Estelle persisted. "Who is this man?"

Florian paused and then said, "I will tell you, but you must never mention it to anyone, Estelle. His name is Orsini."

It meant nothing to her. What was amazing was that there had been all these things going on in their lives about which she had known nothing. But there was still something that puzzled her.

"I think I understand about Cosi, but what I don't see is — why Oriana? What does she care about Napoleon or Eugénie? Or who rules France, and how?"

Florian got up and stretched. "I'm going to order tea, dear girl. I drank too much last night, as you doubtless know." He tugged on the bell-pull and returned to the sofa.

"Oriana, Estelle, is what the French call *une femme maîtresse.*

Unlike Cosi, it is power that fascinates her — over people, over events. In spite of the game you saw her playing, she's only interested in passion as a tool to control other people. At heart, she is a cold woman. Our personal relationship has been over for a long time. It was of brief duration and curiously unsatisfying. I have never understood why, and I don't intend to ponder it any further."

They were interrupted by a powdered, periwigged footman with tea. During the interval of silence caused by the servant's presence, Estelle thought of other questions that needed answers. When the footman had gone, she asked, "Was I simply to be left the run of Aberville House while you were away?"

"Why not? As you see, it virtually runs itself. We had planned to leave a letter for you, suggesting you visit Bostock Hall. You know how calmly your arrival would have been received."

"Who is Orsini?"

Florian's detached air became noticeably more disturbed. "Don't pursue it, Estelle. It would be better if you didn't say the name again, and certainly not in anyone's presence."

"They are plotting again, aren't they? Just as they plotted over me."

He made no attempt to deny it, to spare her feelings. "Yes, they are plotting again, but the stakes are higher this time. That is why you must be quiet."

She felt angry at his sense of priorities. "No stakes seem higher to me than the ones that were played with me, with my life."

"You are right, of course, and I'm sorry. But this could involve danger to our lives if either of us is careless."

With the anger she now felt fear. In the last few minutes, the structure of her life had again been drastically altered. Her private discoveries — the sham of her marriage, the intrigues of the woman she had thought was her friend, her violation by this man — these were now, it seemed, only a small part in a clandestine drama being played on a European stage.

When he spoke again, Florian's tone was light, reassuring. "But you mustn't worry about it, Estelle, because it needn't concern you in the least. It is not part of your life and will only be presumed to be so if you mention to anyone else what I have told you."

As she looked across at him, another question occurred to Estelle, so important to her that she could not ask it. There they were, alone together in this great house for heaven knew how many weeks. What would be the nature of their relationship? Was she to spend night after night denying him, feeling the exhausting conflict of emotions she had experienced the previous night?

She looked at Florian in the darkening library and thought what a picture of domesticity they were, with the tea tray between them and Treasure asleep at their feet. He said nothing at all about the issues that burned between them. Instead, he leaned back on the sofa and held forth at length on the relative virtues of Boucher and Watteau, without making any reference to personal matters or to her appearance on the same sofa as Madame de Pompadour only twenty-four hours before.

Chapter Fifteen

THERE WERE NO GUESTS at Aberville House that evening. Oriana obviously had some swift way of letting her circle know when she was out of the country. Estelle sat in her room and wrote long-overdue letters to oncle Matthieu, Uncle William, and Aunt Dorothea. Then she waited, fully dressed and trembling.

Florian did not appear. Eventually she went apprehensively to bed and woke at daybreak to find herself alone in bed. She wondered if Florian had gone away as well.

He had not. He put in an appearance at breakfast and was his usual languid, courteous self. Then he disappeared for the rest of the day. Estelle dined by herself that evening.

This pattern was repeated for more than a week. They were only together in the presence of servants, and so their conversation was restricted to such matters as the weather, mutual friends, and Treasure's health. Florian obviously felt no need to explain his absence in the evening, since he never mentioned it.

It had become painfully clear to Estelle that she had no personal friends whatsoever. The whole content of her life had been dependent on Cosi and Oriana. Without them, she had no existence at all. Perhaps it was better to have been merely a marionnette dancing at the end of the string they manipulated. At least then she had danced.

As a matter of form, the foursome had usually attended church on Sundays. Now, Estelle started to think again of the vengeful, all-seeing God of her childhood. Maybe this living death was a punishment, but for which of her sins she wasn't sure. She only knew she was experiencing loneliness and fear.

There was a fierce late winter storm about a week after Cosi and Oriana's departure. Even in London the weather was violent, and the winds screamed around Aberville House in a manner worthy of the Channel Islands. The sound added homesickness to Estelle's personal store of pain.

Alone in her room Estelle found herself thinking of what had passed between herself and Florian, something she had not previously allowed herself to do. She had told herself she must put it from her mind, that it would only make her more afraid. It came back to her, as fresh and vivid as if it had just happened — his hands on her breasts, his body pressing her to the bed. A searing flame of sexual longing coursed through her and she shuddered, clutching the arms of the chair in which she sat, close to the fire.

A burst of sleet hit the flames and hissed, spattering small pieces of coal onto the rug at her feet. With a start, Estelle was roused out of her thoughts and she carefully smothered the coals with her shoe. As she watched her foot moving back and forth on the rug before her, the image she had tried to expunge came back with such violence that the pain and hurt lifted her from her chair.

Pulling a shawl around her, not knowing clearly what she was doing or where she was going, she made for the door, heading in the direction of the suite of rooms that had been shared by Florian and Oriana.

She didn't have to look for long. She found Florian in the small sitting room he usually occupied. It was dark, with one lamp lit, and the fire was more soft gray ash than glowing coals.

She could see the decanter at the table near his right hand, a half-filled glass within reach. From the slackness of his body, she could see that he was very drunk.

She came over and knelt down beside him, moving the small table away so that she could get closer.

"Lea' that alone. Wha' ya doin', ya lackey, eh?" His voice was slurred, heavy.

"It's Estelle, not a lackey. At least, I don't think of myself as one, in spite of everything. Why, Florian, why? Have you done this every night or just tonight?"

His head swiveled around with effort and his gaze fixed on her. Then his eyes closed.

"Oh God, not you. Go away, Estelle, go away."

"No, I'm going to call a servant and get you into bed. I'll call Mercer."

He put out a hand as if it weighed a hundredweight and laid it heavily on her arm. "No, no, I'll get there somehow. Poor Mercer — every night. . . . Damned if I wan' — even Mercer t'see me like this again."

He made an effort to sit up on the couch and Estelle took him by the arm. "Jus' a minute, gettin' my bearin's. Don' worry, I'll lean on all the furn'ture — I'm used to it."

Slowly, he felt his way like a blind man along the length of the room, staggering occasionally against Estelle. At the door of the bedroom, he paused for a moment as if gathering strength and made for the bed by the shortest route possible, falling onto it with a groan.

"Made it — leave me now. I'll be all right."

Estelle pulled his feet up onto the coverlet and took off his shoes. He had already removed his collar, so she simply loosened his jacket. Suddenly, he grasped her hand and held it against his chest. She felt his heart beat against her fingers.

"Don' worry, I'll not do anything. You asked why — I'll tell you why. Did it so's not to come after you. Did it to stop thinking of you, to leave you alone."

Incredulously, Estelle looked at him. She could think of nothing to say.

"Go. I'll sleep now." Already, his eyes were closing. Quietly she left the room.

Florian didn't appear at breakfast. Estelle waited until the evening of the next day, just after dinner, which was served to her as usual in lonely splendor by three servants. Then she made her way down the corridors again.

From the look of the decanter, he hadn't yet started. He looked pale but completely sober. His gaze had the disturbing, searching quality she remembered from the early days at Bostock Hall.

"Are you feeling better?" she asked gently.

"Yes, thank you. Why are you here?"

"To be with you. To — stop you drinking."

"You know what I want to stop me drinking."

"Yes, I know."

"Not enough, Estelle. Not enough."

"You need me."

"Not enough, star-lady."

"I need you." Her arms went out to hold him even before he reached her, and she saw the joy in his eyes. Their kiss was mutual for the first time, an exchange of passion, a communication. Then he took her up in his arms and carried her through the bedroom door.

She felt his body against hers with a sense of recognition and welcoming. She heard his moan of pleasure as she parted her thighs to receive him and gasped as she felt the impact of him within her. This time, there was no subjugation, but a wild, mutual ride that carried them along together toward the final climax. As he cried aloud, she felt her own tears on her face. They bore no relation to the tears that had escaped under an orange silk mask more than a week ago.

A warmth that was new to her flooded her body, suffusing her skin with its glow. She sighed and felt his hand stroke her shoulder, his mouth touch her hair. Cradling her head in the curve of his arm, she held him close to her and fell into a deep sleep.

It was a sin. It was adultery — a young girl taken by force and then corrupted for his own pleasure by an older, more experienced man. It was magic and mystery, an overwhelming joy. It was poetry laced with a passion so strong that their obsession became its own justification. They could not have behaved in any other way, and they did not even think of trying.

Estelle moved the few private belongings that gave her a sense of personal identity to Florian's suite of rooms. Finally, she felt she was married.

They were alone, self-absorbed, for three more weeks. One late afternoon, as they sat together on the sofa in the library, where Florian was educating her in the few calm moments that surfaced between great expanses of passion, Oriana and Cosimo appeared in the doorway at the far end of the room.

It was as if they had picked it up from the air. Cosimo's eyebrows went up, and Oriana's full mouth described a downward curve. Without a word, Florian put out his hand and placed it on Estelle's skirt, high on her thigh, where it meets the secret curves of the body. He looked straight up at them.

"Your point is taken, Florian. Well taken." Oriana spoke first. Cosimo opened his mouth, closed it, then suddenly clapped his hands together. He started to laugh, peal upon peal of lively, ringing laughter.

"Bravo, bravissimo! Now that is over, and we can start to build our friendship again!"

Chapter Sixteen

THE FOUR COMPANIONS RETURNED TO PARIS together in the spring of 1857, where France's Second Empire welcomed la Principessa Estella da Gamba with open, perfumed arms.

They stayed in a mansion that Oriana had found for them on her previous visit with Cosimo. It faced toward the Tuileries and overlooked the Seine, glittering with plate-glass windows outside and countless mirrors inside. Among the Corinthian columns, pilasters, and cornices Florian showed Estelle the symbols of the Second Empire: swans, gryphons, palm leaves. Exotic, exciting — as different as her bedroom was from the rose and peach of Aberville House. A silver bed resting on the back of two silver swans dominated the bedroom. The walls were covered in white silk, embossed with blue lace. The great windows were draped with pale-blue silk. The carpet was of the same blue, while all the ornaments and lamps were of silver. Adjoining the bedroom was a bathroom, with a white marble bath sunk into the floor.

Estelle luxuriated in a milky sea of gardenia-scented bubbles up to her chin and marveled that this world could be accommodated on the same planet as Guernsey and Le Refuge. She looked across at Florian, who was watching her from a bergère draped in white muslin, and shuddered as she imagined the eyes of Celestine looking on the same scene.

"What will we do first, Florian?"

"Difficult to decide, my darling. One of the delights of Paris is that one has so little time in which to be bored. Of course, I could be bored anywhere, but you have made that more difficult."

Estelle watched the expression in his eyes as she rose from the scented foam. "Where are Cosi and Oriana?"

The expression changed. "Elsewhere. Best not to ask — nor to know, Estelle."

Estelle shivered and reached out for the wrap he was holding. "Are you part of this, Florian?"

"Inescapably I am, because I was involved at the beginning. I am giving it very little of my attention now. But I must tell you, my love, that if Cosi and Oriana need my help, I shall give it to them."

"Why?" she asked, bewildered. "Do you believe in whatever it is they are doing, or do you need it as a distraction?"

Florian held her against him, stroking her body through the light wrap, pulling the wet fronds of her hair around her face. "My darling, I am bound to them in a way I find difficult to explain. If it weren't for them, I would probably be dead by now. They have indulged my excesses, as they have indulged their own, but they could always manage to stop me before I drove myself too far. They were the only ones . . . until you."

"I don't understand why they pursue something you tell me is so dangerous."

Florian smiled and patted her shoulder. "Cosi is a creature of whim, and this is his fancy for the moment. That can, of course, change at any time. But Oriana — ah, Oriana will not change now. You see, Oriana is determined to alter the course of history. By doing that, she will feel immortal."

The chill which Estelle now felt had nothing to do with damp skin or wet hair. "What in God's name are they thinking of that would be so momentous as that, Florian?"

In answer he held her against him as if he were the one who was cold and she alone could warm him.

"Much can be done in France through the medium of a state ball," said Cosimo, drumming his fingers lightly against the edge of the landau as he gazed out onto night-shrouded Paris streets.

"How wise you are tonight, Cosi!" exclaimed Oriana.

"I cannot in all fairness claim it as my own. I heard one of the emperor's advisors say it last year," said Cosimo. He leaned forward and tapped Estelle's hand. "And you thought such balls were purely for entertainment, didn't you, *cara mia*?"

She withdrew from his touch, as she always did now, burying her hands in the gleaming white satin skirt of her dress. "Yes, if I thought about them at all."

Florian's arm touched hers reassuringly. He was discreet in his behavior toward her when Cosimo and Oriana were present, and she was grateful for it. The last thing she wanted was for her relationship with Florian to feed the voyeuristic tastes of her husband and Florian's wife.

"Cosimo is right," he said. "But that doesn't mean that tonight won't be the most marvelous entertainment. The empress has great style."

"Which is more than one can say for her husband," said Cosimo, his voice dripping with sarcasm. "He has abandoned both artistic and liberal ideals with shameless speed."

This time the arm against Estelle's stiffened, and Florian's voice was cold. "No politics tonight, Cosi. Keep your views out of the Tuileries and the Galérie d'Apollo. There's a good chap."

Oriana put out her hand toward her husband. "Just before we obey you, Florian — a word of advice to you, Estelle. Avoid mentioning the Channel Islands. Many opponents of the emperor are in exile there now. In these troubled times a court official might see intrigue where there was none." Oriana's tone was light, mock-innocent, as she spoke the last words.

Estelle felt a moment's panic. "What about my accent when I speak French?"

Oriana shrugged gleaming white shoulders above the

midnight-blue of her gown. "Only a Channel Islander could place it, my dear, and it's unlikely any will be present."

The landau pulled up to the steps at the Tuileries and a footman opened the door.

Inside the palace the staircase was lined by the magnificent men of Les Cent-Gardes, dressed in blue and silver, chosen for their appearance and presence. There were the diplomatic corps, glittering with gold braid, and the officers of the imperial household, resplendent in their embroidered court dress. Guests with important titles abounded: Maréchal Vaillant, Grand Marshal of the Palace; the Duke of Cambacérès, Grand Master of Ceremonies; the Duke of Bassano, Grand Chamberlain. There were flowers, flowers everywhere, and the sound of harps echoed through the historic halls.

"Dear Lord and Lady d'Aberville, how delightful to see you — and Principe da Gamba!"

A woman had come toward them, wearing the badge of office of the empress's ladies-in-waiting, an "E" in diamonds on blue enamel, with the imperial crown over it.

"Madame la Duchesse, allow me to introduce my wife to you — la Principessa Estella da Gamba. This, my dear, is the Princess of Essling, Grand Mistress of the Empress's Household."

Estelle took the extended hand and sank into a deep curtsy. She wasn't sure if it was the right thing to do, but the Princess of Essling seemed pleased.

"Quite delightful, Principe da Gamba. I must congratulate you both on your marriage and wish you much happiness. I know the emperor and empress would wish to do the same. Come."

She turned and floated ahead of them across the vast floor and they followed. Ahead, Estelle could see a group of imposing men in flowing burnous around two figures.

"Algerian caids — leaders — here on a diplomatic visit," whispered Florian to Estelle. "There are the emperor and empress. Don't worry. He likes pretty women, and she is charming."

Eugénie was more than charming. The empress had, par excellence, what the French call *le sentiment de la toilette.* Her style was hard to define but was superior to any other woman in the room. She wore a mauve moiré dress, diamonds suspended like dewdrops from the gem-flowers in her hair with a panache that was subtle yet striking.

As Florian and Estelle approached, the caids moved back, bowing, and the Princess of Essling flowed smoothly into the gap.

Curtsying was undoubtedly the right thing to do now. As Estelle rose again to her feet and lifted her head, she saw the melancholy eyes of the Emperor Napoleon III upon her. He was quite short in stature, with dark, receding hair, a waxed mustache, and a small beard. He had a strong nose, and there was a feeling of command about the man. The color of his skin, however, suggested someone in poor health or under great stress.

Estelle needn't have worried about what to say, for the imperial couple made it easy. The emperor exchanged some personal remarks with the triumvirate about mutual London friends, while the empress smiled charmingly at Estelle.

Whatever Cosi's declared political stance, he spoke to the emperor with his usual sweetness and charm, reminiscing about the past. Relieved, Estelle glanced sidelong at her husband. At his temple, a pulse throbbed just below the fringe of blond hair. The frenetic tic was at odds with the relaxed cadence of his voice. She was relieved when both protocol and the presence of other guests moved them away from the royal couple.

She saw Florian look at Cosimo, whose hand now beat the same angry rhythm of the silver buttons of his jacket. Cosimo returned his glance and suddenly threw back his head in one of those peals of laughter Estelle had onced loved to hear.

"Enough! Let's enjoy the rest of the evening, *mes amis*! We have paid our respects and thus paid for our pleasures. Now let's take them and forget everything else!"

It was easy to forget during the course of that magical evening. And it was only too easy to forget during the days that followed, for they were caught up in a constant fairyland of bals masqués, entertainments, soirées. Even Florian, who usually became sated with such a sugarplum diet, now saw it through the eyes of another.

They laughed at the farces of Labiche, danced to the music of Offenbach, went to Meyerbeer at the Opéra, saw Rachel and Ristori at the Comédie Française, climbed the brass-tipped stairs of La Maison d'Orée to eat with friends. They were part of the imperial carnival at its zenith, with all the other nations that had gathered to celebrate with them. From Italy, Brazil, Japan, they came from all over the world to enjoy themselves.

When spring turned into summer, Florian and Estelle accepted a royal invitation to Fontainebleau, where they danced on scented, flower-strewn lawns. Before their departure they were invited to visit Compiègne in the autumn.

"A great honor," said Florian. "And now that just leaves us with the summer to fill." They were back in Paris, in their mirrored, marbled palace. Florian's words filled Estelle with sadness. For her, the summer ahead was a treasure box of new delights to be opened, new European cities to explore. Now, suddenly, it became a void to be crossed, covered, somehow consumed.

As she looked at Florian across the great expanse of Aubusson carpet, it struck her that he was drinking more heavily again. The evenings were becoming more frequent when he didn't join her in the blue-and-silver bedroom. She had no qualms about his faithfulness to her, for she knew only too well where he was. He would be in the leather-walled smoking room, amid the red and gold Genoese velvet hangings, a glass in his hand, two decanters on the table before him.

The first time Estelle had found him there, she had laughed and ignored him when he said, "Go away. I'm no use to you tonight." She had gone to him, done the things that he had taught her gave him pleasure. And she had learned, with bitter melancholy, that the golden liquid in the glass before him sometimes had a greater power than her love.

It was time to discuss their summer plans. On a couch close to the fire — for she always felt the cold — Oriana turned and said to Estelle, "My dear, I think we should go our separate ways this summer. You should take Florian to Eauxbonnes in the Pyrenees, for the waters. Cosimo and I have much planning to do — and I have special needs I wish to fulfill this summer. I, too, will take the waters, but elsewhere."

She and Estelle were alone, which happened rarely now. Estelle felt relief at hearing Oriana's suggestion. Perhaps Florian would improve if removed from the influence of his wife and Cosimo. Out of politeness, however, she said, "Can you not take the waters with us, in the Pyrenees?"

Oriana stretched and yawned, clasping her white hands behind her head. "Dearest Estelle, I shall go to Schlangenbad, where they tell me the springs give eternal youth." She rolled over and balanced her chin on the curved brocade arm of the sofa, her mouth tight with the smile that escaped no further than the lips, never to the eyes. "At the beginning of time, great serpents laid their eggs in its bed. They feed the waters and those who take them. I shall need its strength for the months to come."

Serpent-fed waters for this temptress. It seemed fitting.

"Very well," replied Estelle. "I will take Florian to Eauxbonnes."

Even the name comforted her. There, in those good, pure waters, Florian would once again see the world reflected through her eyes.

Chapter Seventeen

FOR A MONTH OR SO, Eauxbonnes won over eau-de-vie. It was enough to be together and to enjoy the scenery, which Florian claimed never to have noticed before, anywhere. "It just lay about one, to be hunted over or crossed en route to somewhere. But it is rather pretty, isn't it?" he drawled, gently mocking Estelle's delighted reception of the grandeur of the Pyrenees.

Estelle had been concerned Florian would miss Cosimo and Oriana, but he rarely mentioned them. He was giving all his attention to educating her in European art, music, literature. He was distracted by her naive enthusiasm, and his physical vigor had returned.

And yet, for all his superior knowledge and experience, Estelle still had the feeling of being Florian's guardian, the one who protected him against the world. As his hand reached out to refill his glass, she would remove it and place it on the curve of her breast. "No, you'll not be able to make love to me tonight."

"Selfish Estelle."

"Self-indulged Estelle, I know — but do you not prefer this,

Florian?" Her hand would reach for his thigh, and she would see the desire in his eyes.

"You know it is — do you know what I wish for, tonight?"

"No. Tell me."

And he would, undressing her as he did so, the decanter forgotten for the time being.

Afterward, she would hold him against her as he slept and think that this was the best moment of all. It was everything to her that he needed her, for he was all she had. Cosi and Oriana were far away, playing with fire. Guernsey had disappeared over some horizon, like a lost dream, and part of that lost dream was Léon de Polnay.

From the Pyrenees, they traveled to the coast, to Biarritz, which was just becoming fashionable since the emperor and empress had purchased a villa there. It was wonderful to be by the sea again, although these waters bore no resemblance to the ocean around her island. Certainly, there were halycon days when Vazon Bay lay calm and blue in the sunlight, but this marine landscape looked as if it had been specially polished and shaped as accessories for the promenades and villas of Biarritz.

Napoléon and Eugénie were not there, however. They were preparing to embark on the *Reine Hortense* for a state visit to Queen Victoria at Osborne House, on the Isle of Wight. It was to be an informal visit between good friends and great sovereigns. Napoleon III was no longer a mere upstart but the most powerful ruler in Europe. Thus he found himself invited to Queen Victoria's favorite summer residence.

And in that Europe across whose summer landscape Florian and Estelle danced, gambled, and made love, there was growing unrest about power being in the hands of this Napoleon. *Napoléon le dernier*, Napoleon the last. *Napoléon le petit*, Napoleon the small. Estelle and Florian's summer playground was a series of disunited kingdoms and republics. Men still remembered Garibaldi riding through Paris on a white horse at the head of 1200 men, a romantic figure with a mane of blond hair, a lasso in his hand, and a blue cloak flying in the wind. The

Romantic writers in Paris gambled, drank, and made love like Estelle and Florian, but they, too, were political animals. They roared about love and life but also grumbled softly — and sometimes not so softly — about the abuse of power, about the lost republic.

Somewhere among the secret societies of Europe — Freemasons, Friends of Truth, Friends of the People, Society of Progress — Oriana and Cosi played very different games. Not for them the gambling salons of Wiesbaden, toward which Estelle and Florian now made their way.

One of the fashionable but well-established watering-spots on the Continent, Wiesbaden had all the charm of an old European city and the freedom of lifestyle to which Estelle was becoming accustomed. In Wiesbaden, she took to wearing more revealing gowns in the summer heat. As men turned to stare at the outline of her body, at the curve of her breasts, she would turn and meet their gaze. There was now a new worldly look to her fresh blond charm. It was an aphrodisiac to Florian d'Aberville when he saw desire in other men's eyes.

She and Florian would laugh together about it in the scented confines of their bedroom. He would take her, saying, "The Duc de Boisvert would like to do this to you," or "The great Graf would have you this way, I think." In the aftermath of one such lovemaking, it occurred to Estelle that she had been made love to by proxy by at least a dozen men in as many days. The thought did not disturb her; that was perhaps the most disturbing thing about it. She was beginning to understand Oriana a little better — or was it that she was becoming more like her?

They saw the summer out in Wiesbaden. All four were to meet again at Aberville House for the opening of the autumn season. They then intended to go to Bostock Hall for the hunting season.

"How long will we stay there, Florian?"

"Until we are bored, star-lady." It was his stock reply to that sort of question. She resolved then and there not to ask any question that might bring that answer. It raised specters that frightened her.

The channel crossing to England was rough, and Estelle thought of the day she had left Saint Peter Port. Would she ever see Guernsey again? Straining her eyes against the spray and fog, she fancied she saw its outline against the wave-swept horizon. She wondered what Léon de Polnay's life was like now. Much of it would be spent on these very seas, and for that alone she envied him. She would not have exchanged his freedom for her own journeying across the face of Europe as the fancy took her, she thought, forgetting that it was not her fancy. It was the whim of a man who was not even her husband, a man to whom she was as bound as if by the bonds of holy matrimony.

As they had done after another European holiday, the couple advanced toward each other across the black-and-white floor of Aberville House. This time, however, the partners were different. Arms outstretched, Cosimo ran gracefully toward his wife.

"*Estella mia,* how beautiful you look! The waters suited you. And Florian, you are looking quite beautiful, too!"

"Estelle suited me," said Florian. He took Oriana's hand and kissed it formally. "The legend of Schlangenbad is no fairy tale, my dear. You look magnificent."

"Thank you, Florian my dear, but what you see here is not serpents' magic. It is the result of a summer ripe with romance and revolution!"

Oriana rolled her r's as the words flowed in her deep, flawed voice. She embraced Estelle, kissing her cheek lightly. Her lips felt hot and dry as if she burned with a fever. "Estelle, you have added sophistication to your youth. You wear your experience like a dress from Palmyre — it adorns you."

"Thank you," said Estelle. She could think of nothing clever or pretty to say, but it was from lack of wanting to rather than lack of words. Picking up her skirts, she moved between them and toward the stairs. At the foot, she stopped and turned back to them, her hand on the banister.

"Romance and revolution, Oriana?" she said. "You seem to

have had a busy summer. I hope you spent my money well." Without looking back, Estelle started up the staircase.

Oriana looked at her husband, her eyes like chips of coal. "What did you tell her?"

"Absolutely nothing. You yourself were foolish enough to use the word 'revolution.' And as for the money — well, she's no simpleton. It didn't take her long to work out what her part was in the scheme of things."

"I am not amused by her insolence. I wonder how she would feel if I told her she was intended as your plaything."

"She already knows that she was supposed to be a *friandise* for me, to be taken and then discarded. But this prolonged summer interlude wasn't planned, was it? I think you allowed it to be in the hopes I would be sated."

Florian's eyes left his wife and he looked toward the staircase. "I have to tell you, my love, that things haven't worked out as you might have expected from my previous reputation. If she is my paramour —" he closed his eyes briefly and opened them again "— then I am, inescapably, her pander."

He looked back at Cosimo and Oriana, smiled, and made his way across the hall.

There was a brief silence, and then Oriana looked at Cosimo. "Jealous?"

Cosimo's pretty mouth twisted and he shrugged his shoulders. A silver trickle of laughter escaped him. "Why should I be? This one has just taken longer, that's all. *Dieu*, if she's so amusing, I can hardly wait until he is able to share —"

He was cut off by Oriana, who had grasped his shoulder so hard that he gasped with pain. "Fool! Don't you see — he's in love with her, and that has never happened before. Florian, you, me. . . . It will never be the same."

Cosimo winced and removed the hand that still gripped his arm.

"Then, dear Oriana, I will be forced to play my trump card, will I not? If I cannot cure Florian, I will have to cure that little *précieuse ridicule* of *her* infatuation, once and for all!"

Oriana's slow smile pulled the red lips wide and tight, pulled the dense white skin into wrinkles that even the serpents of Schlangenbad hadn't been able to banish.

"Of course, Cosi, I had forgotten. She doesn't know that yet, does she?"

Their amusement rang through the hall, echoing back off the Roman centurions on its walls and Aurora and Diana in flight above their heads.

Chapter Eighteen

As was to be expected, Uncle William, Aunt Dorothea, and Bostock Hall were unchanged. When Uncle William greeted them and said, "Ah — ah," Estelle felt an extraordinary affection for him. It could also have been because he threw Cosimo the glance of deep suspicion and undisguised hostility he usually reserved for foreigners.

This time Cosimo seemed disconcerted by it. Even at Aberville House he had been uneasy and restless, as if some pattern in his life had been unexpectedly disrupted. Since he himself had created her role of token wife, Estelle wondered what else had changed.

She knew that Oriana was different toward her since she had spoken her mind that first day back in London. Estelle had no desire to be a leader, but she had drastically altered her role of follower. It was not to Oriana's liking.

The somnolence and otherworldiness of Bostock Hall soothed the tensions that had been mounting among them in London. The rearrangement of the couples did not impinge on the awareness of Uncle William and Aunt Dorothea, whose grip on reality was tenuous at the best of times. No one asked awkward questions, because one mostly talked about hunting.

They rose early and spent most of the day outside in a crisp and glowing autumn that spread golden leaves under their horses' hooyes and carried the scent of cider apples on the air. With Florian by her side, Estelle slept better than she had in months. He would wake her in the night to make love with a tenderness that was oceans removed from the frenetic voyeurism of their European lovemaking. This new eroticism was slow, gentle, and intensely private. Imagined dukes and grafs vanished from Estelle's bedside, and she was relieved to notice that she didn't miss or need their presence.

Then the weather broke. Autumn took on a different odor, of rotten apples decaying in heaps in the orchards and sodden leaves rotting in the mud. Uncle William drifted back to the library. Aunt Dorothea floated back to her aquarium. The two couples returned to London.

Aberville House opened its doors every evening, as it had always done during the winter season, and guests came and went as they had done the previous winter. There were, however, newcomers, strangers to the house, who were received in Oriana or Cosimo's private rooms. Two or three were French. What was more unusual were the Englishmen whose accent and clothing placed them in the lower classes. Yet they were received in the same private rooms as the nobility. They were never announced, and Estelle had not seen them come through the front door, but she was sure their use of a side door was dictated by discretion rather than class. With a sense of unease, she realized that whatever game Oriana and Cosimo had been playing had not been abandoned.

Whatever anxiety Estelle had begun to feel evaporated in the excitement of planning their return to Paris. They were to take a private train out to Compiègne to join the royal party. They would stay there for about two weeks in November, then return to Paris. They would go back to Compiègne for the special hunts around Christmastime, each with its own particular name: *chasse à tir, chasse à cour, chasse aux flambeaux.*

"Is Cosimo such a special friend of the emperor that he receives such invitations, or is it you?" Estelle inquired.

Florian laughed. "The emperor certainly has a feeling of obligation to those who stood by him during his exile, but it's really because the empress loves to invite people who hunt. Many of the guests she entertains there are writers, philosophers, and so on. They are more at home in the grand salon at one of Merimée's spelling-bees than out in the great forests of Compiègne. One 'hallali' from the master of the hunt, and they have difficulty staying with their mount for long."

Florian was drinking again, not to the point of stupor but certainly to greater excess than he had done since the beginning of the summer. Although he spent most of the time with Estelle, there were occasions when he disappeared, and she knew he must have some part in Oriana and Cosi's enterprise.

Her suspicions were confirmed by chance one evening when Estelle was looking for Treasure, who had been given into her charge. Treasure disliked Cosimo and Florian, tolerated Estelle, and was devoted to Oriana. At the turn of a back, he would take off after his mistress, and it could take an hour of wandering through endless corridors and state-rooms to find him again.

Estelle had left her private sitting-room for a moment to fetch something from her adjoining bedroom, only to return to see Treasure trotting smartly out of sight through the open door into the hallway. Exasperated, Estelle started to run after him.

Treasure knew where he was going. He purposefully headed for Oriana's rooms, which were on the same floor but in another wing of the house. Somewhat impeded by her skirts, Estelle ran after him.

She was too late. Ahead she could see Treasure throwing his small body against the closed door of Oriana's room, whining and scratching to get in. Estelle was just about to grab the little dog when the door was opened.

"I'm sorry, Oriana — he got away from me again." Looking up from where she crouched over Treasure, Estelle saw a group sitting around the fire: Florian, Cosimo, Oriana, and a stranger. He was a man of Mediterranean coloring, with dark eyes that looked fixedly at her. They seemed wary rather than hostile.

"My poor Estelle, what a chase Treasure always leads you on!" Oriana stood up and came over, pulling Estelle up none too gently by the arm. She gestured toward the room's interior. "May I introduce a friend of ours, a compatriot of Cosi's: Monsignor Orsini."

The name Estelle was never to say, the man whose existence she must never admit. She gave a small curtsy. "*Enchanté, monsieur.*"

From where he sat the man bowed back but did not rise or speak.

"You can leave Treasure with me, Estelle."

Quite clearly, she was being dismissed. Outside the room, she could hear Florian reassuring the others, "She'll say nothing. She knows that much — too dangerous."

Filled with foreboding, she walked slowly back to her rooms. Would that they were already in Compiègne! And yet — was it not in France that this drama was to be played out, whatever it might turn out to be?

When Florian came to her that night, she did not turn to hold him as she would normally have done. She stiffened when she felt his body against hers, smelled the liquor on his breath.

"Would you like me to explain to you? Would that make it better?" he inquired.

"No. I saw a man who doesn't exist, heard a name I will not recall. That's all."

"That way is best."

"Why can't it be your way, too?"

"I told you why."

"Am I not enough?"

"Star-lady, I wish you were." Florian's arm came around her waist and reached for her hand. She took it and held it against her, and heard his sigh of pleasure. If this was all she had, it was better than nothing, better than Oriana's discordant laugh and empty friendship, better than the extravagant gaiety of her hollow, mock-husband.

In the great forest of Compiègne, the hunt met at the King's Well. Eight magnificent alleys pierced through a plantation of oak trees, where the Forest Guards waited on the huntsmen. Their coats were green, French cut; they had high yellow gaiters, pointed hats, and hunting knives at their belts. The Prince of the Moscowa, Master of the Imperial Hounds, wore red livery. Whether for stag or for boar, the hunt was always organized to perfection.

Afterward, punch was served in the clearing and the party returned to Compiègne by torchlight. Empress Eugénie was then at her most beautiful and vivacious, laughing and joking with her guests, riding her horse with superb Spanish panache.

In the mornings there were expeditions to such scenic spots as Mont Berry and the Chateau de Pierrefonds; in the afternoon, tea in the salon, with the likes of Gounod the composer, the great scientist Pasteur, the writer Alexandre Dumas; in the evening, theatre, with actors from the Opéra and the Comédie Française.

There were actors playing gentlemen, and gentlemen trying to be actors. Reality forgotten; intrigue forgotten. The jealous exclusiveness of the royal circle that had made it suspect had also made it vulnerable. It had forgotten to look beyond the Gobelin tapestries of Compiègne, the orangerie terrace of the palace of Saint-Cloud, the Porte-Dorée at Fontainebleau.

Estelle, too, had forgotten. She even found Cosi and Oriana amusing once more.

The two couples returned, reluctantly, to spend Christmas in England and to make the obligatory visit to Bostock Hall. By the end of December they were back in Paris, in the mansion that looked toward the Tuileries, where the emperor and empress were again in residence.

Things were not as they had been, however. The carnival

atmosphere had gone; the concealed faces of the men who came and went through the Corinthian pillars were not masked for amusement but hooded against recognition. There was a feeling of urgency in the air, and Estelle was aware that whatever was being planned was close to execution.

One night, the faceless men did not leave until dawn. As Estelle sat in Florian's dressing-room waiting for him, she heard their voices murmuring down the long corridors, menacing as a threatening storm.

When he finally came through the doors, his face was gray with fatigue. "Estelle, you shouldn't have waited up for me."

"I decided to because I couldn't sleep."

He came over to the sofa on which Estelle sat, knelt down and buried his face in her lap, stroking her thighs through the soft silk of her robe. "I'm glad, though I'm damn tired."

"I waited to talk, not to make love." She touched his hair, felt that strong maternal pull that had bound her to him from the first.

"I'm too tired to talk, star-lady."

"It will be too late if we don't talk now." Estelle pulled away from him, clasping her hands in her lap. "Florian, you have helped them in whatever it is. I know the moment is near, and whatever you have planned will be carried out soon. I'm asking you to leave right now, come back to England with me. If you don't, I shall leave on my own. Once I am there, I shall stay by myself. I shall return to Bostock Hall, and you will never see me again."

It hurt her to say it. Could she really live a life of buttony again? She saw him clench his hands, heard the pain in his voice.

"Are you threatening me, Estelle?"

"I have to, for both of us. I have a feeling that if you stay in Paris what has been will never be again."

Florian rose slowly from his kneeling position and slumped on the far end of the sofa. He said nothing for a moment, and she could feel the tension make her heart thump. Then he said, "Maybe you're right, star-lady. What more do they need me for? I hadn't planned to be there, anyway, when . . . it happens. Yes, yes," he repeated, rubbing his eyes with his knuckles, like a small child. "We could go back, wait for them in London."

She felt joy, an overwhelming sense of relief. "I'll make the arrangements, Florian. You sleep now. They won't care, you'll see. We'll tell them tomorrow."

He was already asleep when she left him, breathing slowly and deeply as if an enormous weight had been lifted from him. She felt so herself, as feather light as the soft down on one of the swans so beloved of the Second Empire.

Chapter Nineteen

WHEN SHE AWOKE, a wintry sunlight was already slanting across the lush carpet of her bedroom. It was not, however, the light that had disturbed her. It was a voice, high and harsh and angry, calling her name. She was confused at first, thinking they were back in England, as they had been in her dream, and that she heard the rooks calling in the elms around Bostock Hall.

"Estelle — Estelle! Wake up — get up!"

She sat up in the silver swan bed, her senses gradually coming back to her, and took in the figure of Cosi standing at the foot of the bed. It was the first time he had ever been in her bedroom, and his presence was as surprising as the anger on his face, the rage in his voice. He was not yet dressed but wore a green velvet robe swathed around him. His usually carefully arranged hair was tousled.

"Cosi, what are you doing here?"

There was no sweetness now, no merry laughter. "I'm your husband, *cara*. Remember?"

Estelle's apprehension quickly changed to distaste. "I

remember . . . and I don't remember. My bedchamber has never been to your liking. Why should it be any different now?"

She reached out for her wrap, which lay on a stool near the bed, but Cosimo was there before she could reach it, grasping her wrist. "No, you listen to me — You have done damage, untold damage, meddled in affairs that don't concern you!"

"I see." So that was it. Florian had already spoken to him. "What difference will it make to your plans if Florian and I go back to England? You don't need him here. And you certainly don't need me, Cosi, do you?"

His mood changed again. She could still feel the underlying anger, but now there was something else. It was almost as if he were mocking her, gloating over some private knowledge.

"No, I don't need you and never have — except for your money, of course. You already know that. If you removed that gown and lay before me naked, you could not excite me. But Florian, now — ah, I *do* need him here."

Estelle felt lost, bewildered by his tone. "Why do you need him here? Has he such an important role in your plans? Let him return to England with me. You have my money."

Cosi was really enjoying his secret joke. The laughter bubbled from him as he replied, "True, so it's just as well you don't care. But Florian? Ah, that's a different matter, and I'm damned if you'll take him away from me. You were meant to be a diversion, an interlude, and then all would be as it was before. Maybe even more amusing, if we could have persuaded you to play our little games. We could have shared Florian then, but you are so possessive of him. And now you would take him back to England! *Dio mio,* enough is enough — I want what was mine!"

His voice rose again, the cry of a spoiled child who has been thwarted, a lover denied.

A lover denied. Much of her innocence had gone in listening to them discuss the world around her, hearing their conversation. No, she couldn't believe it, wouldn't. Her loathing shivered through her voice.

"You are obscene, Cosi. Would you have me think that you were — that he — that —"

"You cannot put it into words, can you? Of course we were! Again and again and again! It pleased Oriana, set her free to do other things. We found it amusing to talk of these things together — Oh, the laughter we shared! You think you're so special to him? *Cara mia,* this is what he once found beautiful!"

Standing before her, legs apart, he tore open the velvet robe and Estelle saw her husband naked for the first time. He was white-skinned, almost hairless, slender. She was reminded not even so much of a young man's body, but of a white and unusually hairless lap-dog owned by a friend of Oriana's. She felt the nausea rise in her throat. The voice railed on and on, trembling with excitement.

"He wasn't the first — there had been so many by that time — but he was the best. So insatiable, so ineffably corrupt! Anything, he would say, so long as he wasn't bored. And I was so happy to oblige my world-weary English milord! Let me tell you what we used to do —" Incredibly, she saw that his body had started to react to remembered perversions, past corruption.

"No!" Desperately, she threw herself off the bed, started toward the door. As if in answer to a prayer, the door opened. Florian was standing there. Cosimo da Gamba smiled and dropped his velvet robe to the floor.

"*Floriano mio,* just in time. Let's show my wife — oh, forgive me, your mistress — what we can to together."

She thought Florian was about to kill him, the rage on his face was so terrible. He swayed, clenched his fists at his side, then walked across the room and picked up the discarded gown.

"Get out. Get out before I kill you."

As if they had had a slight tiff, a minor disagreement, Cosi pouted and shrugged his shoulders. "Very well, *Floriano mio.* I'll leave you to explain how things really are." He took his robe from Florian and swung it nonchalantly round his shoulders. *"Adieu, à bientôt."* With a graceful bow to each of them, he left the room.

"My darling Estelle." Florian held out his arms to her, his face a mask of agony. "He is a monster."

She felt as if she had swallowed a sorbet ice too fast and a piece had stuck in her throat. "So are you. Go back to them, where you belong."

"But I don't, I know that now. I belong with you." She could hear the terrible despair in his voice, but it didn't move her.

"Never. You are as tainted as they are." Looking straight at him, Estelle spoke the words flatly, cold as the ice inside her. "Your body disgusts me. I don't want you any more."

Florian looked at her for a moment. Then he bowed, turned on his heel, and left the room. Estelle watched his hand finally disappear around the door as he closed it behind him, the hand that had caressed and delighted her. She felt the ice settle somewhere around her heart.

Estelle stayed in her suite of rooms all morning. At about midday, Oriana arrived unannounced, with Treasure in her arms. She seemed unconcerned, as buoyant as ever.

"Estelle, my dear, are you unwell? Why have you been hiding yourself away?"

"You don't know?"

"What don't I know, my dear?" There was something about her artless inquiry that made Estelle quite sure Oriana knew precisely what.

"You will not be unhappy to hear that the liaison with Florian is over. I wish to return to England as soon as possible — tomorrow, the day after, if I can. I will need your help to arrange it."

"Oh, Estelle!" Oriana sank in graceful surprise onto the sofa, and placed Treasure at her feet. "Of course, if you wish to return to England, I won't stop you — much as I would miss you." A white hand lay heavily for a moment on Estelle's arm and then was withdrawn. "We'll see what we can do tomorrow. But of course you will attend the Opéra tonight, won't you? I will make the arrangements with so much better grace if you say yes!"

Oriana was making no real attempt to conceal her threat.

"Very well," Estelle replied. "But I will eat in my room this evening."

Oriana shrugged her shoulders and stood up. "If you insist. I will see you tonight." There was amused contempt on her face as she added, "After tonight, Estelle, you may feel differently about . . . everything."

"Never. That can never be."

"Nothing is forever, so one can never say never." Oriana's lighthearted attitude suddenly left her, and there was a steely quality to her voice. "The course of human history is so much more important than one's own small disappointments. You'll see that, Estelle, when you walk in its shadow."

Without further explanation, she scooped up Treasure and left the room.

The terrible emptiness of the day dragged past. Sleep was impossible, for it brought images of Cosi's naked white body, the sound of his triumphant laughter, the truth on Florian's face. Better to sit staring into the distance, allowing her maid to choose her clothes, dress her hair, prepare her for the evening's entertainment. This was a farewell performance at the Opéra by the great baritone, Massol, which was to be attended by the emperor and empress. It was a gala event: Massol was to perform the second act from *William Tell.* The arrangements were that Oriana and Estelle would go together, while the two men, who had some sort of dinner to attend at the Jockey Club, would meet them afterward at the Opéra.

Oriana was late for their departure, offering no explanation when she finally arrived. Her *beauté de diable* was even more breathtaking than ever, a glitter of excitement like a patina over her serpent stare. *"Chère Estelle, allons-y!"* Her smile washed over Estelle with ill-disguised contempt.

Wordlessly, they sat opposite each other in the carriage. Outside the window, Estelle could see a troop of the Lancers of the Guard, as they rode up the rue de Pelerier, clearing the way for the royal landau. She and Oriana were obviously arriving just ahead of the emperor and empress, which was unusually late for them.

They reached the curb of the peristyle outside the Opéra just before the royal carriage, and Estelle prepared to get out as their own carriage slowed down.

"No — wait a moment." In the semi-darkness Oriana's eyes were gleaming more feverishly then usual, her breathing rapid and shallow."We are late," she said. "Let them enter first."

"But we'll —" She was just about to sit back again, when there was the sound of a violent explosion. Estelle was thrown forward against the seat opposite. She had only time to open her mouth to cry out, when two more explosions sounded. Temporarily deafened, she looked sideways out the carriage window and saw the gas jets on the Opéra facade blow out.

"My God, they're too close! They're mad!" Oriana threw herself on the floor of the carriage and clapped her hands over her ears.

Estelle couldn't hear the words, but the shout was enough. She flung herself at the carriage door and out into the street and a mob that screamed and seethed and surged around her.

A scene of chaos and carnage met her eyes. There was broken glass everywhere, people running and screaming. The imperial carriage lay crazily tilted, its wheels blown off. The great horses that had drawn it lay on the ground, either dead or dying. One, with its head lifted in the air, mouth open, made a horrific whinnying sound. A cocoa-seller, his little barrel still close to him, lay screaming a few feet from Estelle in a pool of blood, his leg blown from his body. One of the royal party, in the dress uniform of a general of the imperial army, was sprawled not far from the royal carriage, blood spurting from a hideous wound in his neck. The crowd awaiting the arrival of the royal party was devastated by the blast.

Estelle could see no sign of Napoleon, but there was a knot of police and soldiers gathered around someone to the side of the landau. A figure in a white dress emerged from the group:

it was Eugénie, white as her dress, blood-stained, eyes staring in shock. For a moment, her gaze met Estelle's across the tangled mass of bodies. Then she turned and was led in the direction of the Opéra, surrounded by soldiers.

Suddenly Estelle heard the scream. It was high and shrill and terrible, primal as the shriek of the wind around her native island. She turned back toward her carriage and saw Oriana bending over something on the roadway. She screamed without cease as she stared at the object before her.

Cosi. At least, from the clothes it was Cosi. He adored that particular jacket, and those were his rings. His shirt had ripped open with the blast, and Estelle could see that strangely hairless body again.

But his face, she thought. Where was his face? Some fair hair left — yes, it must be Cosi — but the face was gone. Gone were the eyes that had wooed her at Bostock Hall, the mouth that had bubbled laughter and lies, and unwanted truths. Just torn flesh — all that was left now of the pretty face of her husband, the looks that had lured Florian — and then her — into seduction, corruption, and treachery.

Chapter Twenty

THEY TOOK ESTELLE BACK to the island — oncle Matthieu and a relative from Saint-Malo. They took her away from the women's prison of Saint Lazare, where she had been incarcerated. Estelle would never remember the prison even when her memory had returned, nor the madwoman she had been when released in a merciful gesture by the authorities. She would later discover that Florian and Orsini — the man whose name and face she wished she had never known — had convinced the police of her innocence.

By the time they got her back to Le Refuge, she was quieter, more manageable. During the day, she would sit staring into the distance for hours on end. The nights were worse. They gave her chloral to drive her into the depths of unconsciousness that lay below dreaming.

Gradually, she returned to some semblance of a normal person, even if that person was not the Estelle her relatives had known. They were glad her memory had gone, because they feared that the madwoman who raved and tore at her hair and face would return with it. So they covered the mirrors, since the reflection of faces seemed to terrify her, and swore everyone to silence.

Three months later, Estelle stood at her open bedroom window and understood why. As they paraded before her — Florian, Cosimo, Oriana — she was shaken to the depths of her being by an emotion that seemed more than distaste of her part, however passive, in treachery and murder, more than horror at the hideous faceless image of her dead husband. She wanted to weep for the ignorance that had betrayed her and given control of her life into the hands of others. She ached at the loss of an innocence that was only partly to do with her rape by a man she still could not hate. Because of the company she had kept, she felt she would be tainted forever.

Other memories had also returned: of the betrayal that had led to her visit to England and the train of events that had followed. Did the roots of her suffering go back to Léon de Polnay, she wondered. Should she hate him for that? No, that wasn't possible. The Estelle of the newly found present understood only too well why he had done it. She no longer believed in the deep dungeons of Castle Cornet for acts such as he had been guilty of.

Where was Florian, she wondered. Had he been executed? The thought filled Estelle with horror, making her realize she was still bound to a man who had taken her innocence and connived at murder. What she felt was grief and pity for the man who had put his arms around her and had filled the emptiness of her life. She knew she must find out what had happened to him, or she would ever be the debtor, haunted by her conscience.

Sitting at the window of her bedroom, the Estelle of the present looked at the newly discovered Estelle of the past and knew there was no going back. She now realized she had imagined that the return of memory would somehow bring that lost Estelle back to her. Her innocence was gone forever, as was the dream that had been part of it: a life with Léon de Polnay.

She could not abandon Florian d'Aberville. When she held Florian close in her arms against the emptiness of his life that could only be filled by her — or by liquor — the emotions that had stirred her were stronger than the dreams of her lost childhood, whether or not she wanted it that way.

Against the rough frame of the window she crossed her arms, put down her face, and wept. These tears were the last she would shed in remorse for past acts. What a tragi-comedy, she thought, that the upbringing that had made her vulnerable also gave her a sense of commitment to the man who, she had been taught to believe, must have doomed her forever as a lost soul!

Glancing up, she saw the lights in the harbor below and the flickering light off Jethou. With the return of memory, she realized she knew who the spirit of la Rocque Varou was. A feeling of excitement hit her. Victor Hugo — poet, romantic, political exile. One of the lions who had roared against that same Napoleon whose existence had so dramatically altered her own life. She, too, was like an exile on her own island.

It was highly likely that such a man would have heard of the attempt on the emperor's life and could answer some of her questions. She would confide in no one but make her own decisions. The thought that she was about to do something independently of anyone else gave her pleasure.

The sea was a May-time blue, creaming gently around the rocks below la Rocque Varou. Estelle remembered Biarritz, the Pyrenees, and resting her head on Florian's shoulder after they had made love. She leaned against the great menhir, lifted her face to the sun, and waited for him to come. When the shadow fell across her shoulder, she knew who it was before she opened her eyes.

"My past has returned to me, and I know who I am," she said.

"I, too. I knew there was some thread that bound us together."

She opened her eyes suddenly and surprised the look of desire on the poet's face. "Why do you look at me like that?" she asked.

He shrugged his shoulders and sat down beside her, throwing back his cloak. "I look at all beautiful women like that. And because I am a poet and a genius, most of them give themselves to me."

"*Quel compliment!*" Estelle started to laugh, amused by the simplicity of his response. Her companion was not in the least put out by her laughter. "Why not? What better reason to make love in this world than to feed genius and be enriched in one's turn?"

"Do you never tire of it, never become weary of persuasion?"

"I never persuade, and I am never bored." His eyes were remarkable: penetrating, perennially young.

Estelle came abruptly to the point. "I'm glad you know who I am, because I have come to you for help. My family doesn't yet know that my memory has returned, but I'm sure they wouldn't help me. You still have contacts with other emigrés, friends in Paris. If you know who I am, you know of the assassination attempt, and my . . . involvement. I know what happened to my husband, but I would like to know what happened to the others."

"The others," he repeated. "Yes, I have indeed heard of what happened. My friends in Paris would have told me anyway of an attempt on Louis Napoleon's life, but the involvement — however marginal — of a Guernsey girl was of particular interest to me. I presume you were there as an innocent bystander?"

"I knew nothing — nothing!" she cried passionately. "Oh, I knew they were conspiring about something, but they were so frivolous, so — so pleasure-seeking, that I never for a moment thought it would be something so terrible! I heard the name 'Orsini' in England and saw him once, but it meant nothing to me. More than that I never knew."

"Well, Orsini was indeed the mastermind, with the help of some other men in Britain. Your aristocratic friends were useful to him, but peripheral. The Abervilles are in prison in Paris, as is Orsini. They had a brilliant lawyer, monsieur Favre, but Orsini is sentenced to death and your friends to imprisonment. There has been some talk of leniency for monsieur d'Aberville, because he was not present at the attempt, and because of his health."

"And they still sentenced him?"

"I am told he was incriminated by his own wife."

"Ah, Florian!" The cry burst from her.

Her companion looked sharply at her. "Ah, I see. You were his mistress."

She shook her head vehemently. "You don't understand. My husband was never my husband. I only belonged to Florian. He alone was my husband!"

"Hmm. If this is hard for me to understand, one can see why Madame d'Aberville might have had difficulty, too. I imagine *she* thought of herself as his wife."

"Never, she —" Estelle found she didn't even want to explain. "None of this is important any more. Is Florian d'Aberville very ill?"

"Liver, I am told. There's no one too interested in pleading his case, now that a great lawyer has failed. The English won't risk it, because relations between France and England are very strained as a result of the affair. The bombs seem to have been manufactured in Britain, and much of the planning went on there."

"I know." He looked at her sharply but didn't press her when she stayed silent. Around them, birdsong filled the air, joining the cries of the gulls. As a cloud crossed the sun, Estelle shivered.

"Here, let me put my cloak around us both. Lean on me, young woman, for me as much as for you. Remember, I never persuade."

She felt the rumble of laughter in the powerful body, the strength of the arm around her shoulders. He continued, "We have dealt with the facts, but how can I help you?"

"I want to get Florian d'Aberville out of Paris."

When the poet replied, his voice was sad. "I would probably do more harm than good. My position vis-à-vis Napoléon le petit is poor, and my friends could be of little help to your cause. I do, however, have a suggestion for you. My friends tell me that monsieur d'Aberville is more often in hospital than in prison. It's much easier to bribe prison guards, to whisk him away in such a situation. Your best ally would not be me in such an enterprise, but the young man of whom you spoke to me once. He will have the necessary contacts, a boat, a skill for concealment. Once smuggled out, I don't think there would be much of a hue and cry. An example had to be made, but I have the impression Monsieur d'Aberville is an embarrassment now." He paused, and said reflectively, "There is only one problem."

"It seems to me I have many, but which one in particular?" Estelle felt him rumble with laughter again.

"*Belle femme,* you have to persuade one gentleman to get the other one out. An interesting dilemma, is it not?"

"Everyone has his price, monsieur."

"*Absolument.* But will you pay it?"

"I will offer him two things."

"Which are?"

"He wronged me in the past, and now he wants me. I will offer him freedom from guilt . . . and promises."

"Absolution now and consummation later. Are you a woman of your word?"

"I don't know. That is his gamble." Hers, too, she thought. Was it safe to offer promises to a man whose touch had inflamed her even when she was innocent? Absolution was easy; she had already given him that before he had promised her anything. Consummation she could not — would not — think about. Estelle moved slightly away from the sheltering arm. "I must go now."

She got slowly to her feet, smoothing down her heavy skirt, looked briefly out toward Jethou, where the light had flickered again in the night. "Monsieur Hugo, tell me one thing."

"If I can."

"You say that relations between England and France are strained, but would you say that this act changed the course of history?"

"No. Of that I am sure."

There was pleasure in hearing him say it. "Poor Oriana."

"The course of history is more often changed by acts of creation than acts of destruction."

"I wish I could believe that. *Adieu,* and thank you."

He watched her go across the sedge and heather toward the path that led to the harbor and the town below.

Such a crazy plan, she thought, that it would be better to act now before I think of any more difficulties. The *Nerine* was there, at its customary moorings. She would beard the lion in his den, before she got cold feet.

To her relief, the young boy who had ferried her out the first time was at the quayside, sitting on some steps cut into the side of the jetty.

"Hola!" she called. "Will you take me out again to the *Nerine*?"

The boy jumped when he heard her voice and hurried to meet her. "I could, madame, but Léon de Polnay is not on board. He is at le clos de Polnay."

"At his house?" Of course, he didn't live on board — she hadn't thought about that. The boy saw the disappointment on her face and said, "I can get you a ride there if you want. My uncle works in les Halles and lives quite close to the de Polnays. He usually leaves for home around this time, and he could take you there."

"I would be grateful." She gave the boy a few coins and he grinned and darted off in the direction of the market. A few minutes later, he had returned with a large countryman of florid complexion, carrying a sack over his shoulder.

"Estelle Gastineau! *Nennin*, I wouldn't have believed it if le petit Jean hadn't told me it was so. Do you remember me — Maturin l'Eustace? Of course, I'll take you to Saint Martin's. Come, I've done what I need for the day."

Estelle pressed a few more coins into le petit Jean's willing hand. "Go and tell Celestine Falla at Le Refuge where I have gone, and tell her not to worry about me," she told him. The lad took off like a shot from a cannon, while Estelle followed her escort to a pony and cart in the open area near the town church. He helped her into the seat and jumped up alongside her, throwing his sack into the cart behind them.

"En avant!" He clicked his tongue and touched the sturdy pony with his whip. Slowly they moved out of the town and toward the neighboring parish of Saint Martin's, which lay to the south of Saint Peter Port. As they jolted over the rough country lanes, passing the *courtis,* the small walled fields of Guernsey, her escort alternately whistled through his teeth and regaled her with details of the ownership and history of each parcel of land they passed.

About his passenger and her own strange history he showed no interest. Island matters were of more interest to him than anything that happened beyond its waters. Estelle felt it was more out of politeness than curiosity when he turned to her and asked, "Why do you visit young de Polnay? His mother is dead now, you know, and he lives on his own."

"I need his help in a matter of some urgency."

"Ah." They were passing the parish church of Saint Martin's as Estelle replied, and Maturin l'Eustace held out his whip and pointed at the gates as they went by. "There — maybe you should bring some flowers to la Gran'mère du Chimquière. She could be more help than de Polnay."

In the churchyard gateway, Estelle could see a worn stone figure, taller than herself, rectangular to the shoulders, but with molded breasts and what looked like the rough outline of hands folded beneath. There was a primitive strength to the face, a stoic impassivity in the gaze that had watched over Saint Martin's for millennia.

"Maybe I will do that."

"Good — it does no harm to have her on your side. In the month of May, *les pouques* — the little people — are everywhere. And, of course, those . . . *personnes-là de tchi qu'nou n'dit rian.*"

"Those people of whom one says nothing? Ah, yes, witches."

Only half the word escaped Estelle, for Maturin l'Eustace

put up his hand as though he would stifle the sound of her voice. "Don't say it! Who knows who is listening!"

His hand moved back to touch some charm that hung on a cord around his neck. "They are everywhere. Sometimes they come in shapes that deceive." He touched the charm once more, before taking the pony's reins again.

How well she knew that, thought Estelle. Beautiful, seductive, and corrupt — Cosimo . . . and Oriana.

They reached the top of a small hill. Below them was a green valley that opened on one side to what Estelle supposed was the shoreline. As they came down the incline into the valley, there was a honeyed warmth in the air.

"This is beautiful. I think I remember it."

"Of course, you do," said her companion with reproof in his voice. "Moulin Huet is over there — and there's le clos de Polnay."

Estelle could see the house now, and as she did so, memories came flooding back. She remembered a laughing, joking little boy and a warm and tender woman who had hugged and kissed her and called her *"ma petite étoile."* Little star. Starlady.

Estelle closed her eyes. Would one memory always return to sully the other?

Along a winding pathway, through the *courtis* of the de Polnay family, they approached the house she had once thought of as her second home.

Chapter Twenty-one

THE HOUSE WAS AS SHE REMEMBERED IT. Through the centuries the original fifteenth-century structure had been added to. The low, square form with the narrow windows adjoined the familiar two storeys of the traditional Guernsey farmhouse, with its sash windows and central doorway. The doorway was well-proportioned, framed by the double Guernsey arch, its stones flush with the surrounding wall.

At the head of the granite arch, Estelle could see the armorial device of the de Polnay family and, above the roof, the turret at the back of the house. She remembered running up the flight of steps outside the house that led through the turret to the second floor. A rose climbed in exotic profusion around the arch and the lower windows, its scarlet blooms splashed across the soft gray stone.

There was no one in sight, but a large dog of indeterminate breed was chained to a ring near the front door. He broke into frenzied barking, baring his teeth at them as the cart came to a halt in the courtyard.

"Watch him, madame. They say he has killed a man. Stay

here, and I'll go round to the back. He'll have my hand off if I go for the knocker on that door."

Maturin l'Eustace got off the cart on the side farthest from the dog and disappeared around the side of the house. Estelle looked apprehensively down at the animal frothing at the wheels of the cart and prayed that the chain was as strong as it looked. As he looked up at her, a name slipped effortlessly into her mind.

"Ranulph — here, Ranulph!"

The barking and growling stopped, and the great dog looked up warily at her. Not a little dog any more, but obviously the same one. He had been a puppy when last she saw him, chewing on old shoes and yapping at the servants' heels.

"*Pas petit chien, eh,* Ranulph? *Gros chien, grand chien,*" she cooed at him, bending cautiously over the side of the cart. A whine escaped Ranulph, and imperceptibly his tail began to wag.

"He remembers you."

Léon de Polnay stood framed in the doorway, his head barely clear of the arch. "What is more, you remember him."

"Yes, I remember."

She saw him again with the eyes of a child: his open, frank countenance, his unruly dark hair ("Léon, don't you ever comb your hair?" "*Bien sur,* Estelle, but it has a life of its own, as I do."); his lean, strong build ("If you grow any more, Léon, you'll be a bean-pole." "All the better to reach up and snatch the hen with the golden eggs, *petite fille*!"); the irresistible smile ("Your teeth are white as pearls, Léon." "I exchanged my real teeth for these in the south seas.")

Gone was her body's response to his looks, the urge that at their previous meeting had made her want him so immodestly. At the thought, she felt the hot flush of horror that stained her cheeks.

"You remembered, and yet you came to see me."

"I remembered, and that's why I came to see you."

His reply was flippant, but she could see that he was genuinely discomfited. "Shall I need Ranulph to protect me?"

"Probably not. Even without Ranulph, you are better protected than I have ever been."

She turned to Maturin l'Eustace, who had reappeared around the side of the house. "I'm very grateful to you, monsieur l'Eustace. May I pay you for your trouble?"

Maturin l'Eustace looked quite put out. "But of course not. May the time never come when I'll not do a favor for a Gastineau or a de Polnay."

Still wary of Ranulph, he helped Estelle out of the far side of the cart and got back into the driver's seat. With a click of his teeth and a flick of the whip, he was gone down the winding driveway.

As the sound of the wheels died away, Estelle turned back and looked at Léon de Polnay. "You are as I remembered you."

"I haven't changed?"

"Not really. Your face bears more marks of wind and weather, that's all."

"That 'all' is much in your case, Estelle. Yours bears marks of weathering that I can only guess at."

Her smile had no joy in it. "You need guess no longer. I came to tell you all."

She detected what she could have sworn was pain in his expression. "There's no need."

"Yes!" Ranulph reacted to the anger in Estelle's voice, and moved closer to his master's side. "This is the price I exact, Léon, for what you did to me. You must bear my burden, for it's partly your doing."

"I'm not responsible for whatever it is that happened to you. I have had no part in your life."

"Precisely. That's why you can play a part in it now. You owe me something for what you did . . . and didn't do!" No, she no longer really believed that, but she had to make him accept it was true.

He reacted as he reacted to any threat, with defiance. "And what if I say I won't do it?"

Memories again, of a little brown-skinned boy defying the servants, hands on skinny hips. "And what if I *won't* do it?"

"Le barbou t'attrapera," Estelle heard herself saying. It was the old childhood threat: the bogeyman'll get you. She felt the laugh rise in her throat, and it was out before she could stop it, piercing clear and true through the anger.

Léon responded with hands held up in mock horror. "Ah, how could you! The most devilish threat of all. You are unscrupulous, without mercy!"

Their laughter joined in the honey-sweet air, and Ranulph jumped up at his master, disturbed as dogs often are by laughter.

"All's well, Ranulph. We'll take this devious woman inside and hear what else she has in store for me."

He unleashed the dog, stood to one side, and allowed Estelle to precede them into the house.

The room was unchanged from her childhood memory of it: solidly and well furnished as befitted the home of one of the *chefs de famille,* yet with the traditional features of humbler island homes. There was the *lit de fouaille,* where Estelle remembered Léon's mother and grandmother sitting on winter evenings before the deep, wide fireplace, the stools still set for the men. There were other lamps in the room, but the Guernsey crasset hung suspended from hook and cord, waiting to be filled with oil and lit against the lengthening evening shadows.

"I loved your mother."

"I know, and she knew it, too. If it gives you any consolation, she never forgave me for what I did to you. Things were never the same between us again."

"I'm sorry about that. It gives me no pleasure at all."

Léon de Polnay shrugged his shoulders. "It's a cross I'll have to bear, like the one I bear because of you."

"Maybe I can offer you an easing of both burdens, if you help me." As she pulled off her cloak and laid it over a stool, tiredness overcame her. It had been the longest, most demanding day she had spent in many a month, and her body ached. She sank gratefully into a chair and leaned her head back.

Léon de Polnay looked at the milky gleam of the curve of her throat, the movement of her hands against the slim waist of her dress, and wondered if she were here for his help or for other things. There was an air of abandonment about her that excited him and yet moved him as well in a less superficial way. She seemed infinitely, achingly vulnerable. He felt an inconvenient rush of pity and hastened to stifle it.

"I'll ask Marie to bring us something to eat. Are you hungry?"

She answered as if surprised. "Yes, I am."

"Then we might as well have our evening meal together."

"Will I remember Marie?"

"No. Old Jeanette died, and I had to let the young servants go — for my sake and theirs. My reputation, you know."

An old countrywoman, dressed in black, served their meal with a noticeable lack of comment or glance toward her visitor. They ate fresh fish, vegetables from the garden, and the soft breadcake the islanders call *galette*.

"I've asked Marie to prepare some mulled wine to fortify us against the revelations that are to come." It was lightly said, but Léon's eyes were serious. "Come, I'll light the fire, and we'll drink it over here."

The old woman served them at the settle by the fire, bringing in the steaming mulled wine in a silver claret jug and setting it on the hearth before them.

"Marie seems undisturbed by my presence."

"She has learned to be undisturbed by anything in this house. She is more put out at serving you milk-à-punch, but she doesn't know this is a sort of celebration — for me, at least."

"It tastes different from what I remember and from what I had in England."

"Of course! This is special to the island. It has ampurdam, claret, spices, and sugar. Hot, strong, and sweet. You were such a good girl before you left here, you had probably only had the tiniest of sips."

"I was good, wasn't I?"

"Perfection, impossible to live up to — for me, at least."

"Don't worry, the same cannot be said now."

He leaned back against the settle and looked at her. As the

flames in the fireplace caught the fresh wood and leaped higher, her face appeared to him as a study in contrasts: sweet mouth, but with a wry twist to it; pure blue of the eyes, haunted by the dark hollow beneath; the high line of the cheekbone shadowing the delicate jaw.

"Take some milk-à-punch and tell me what happened to you after you left the island."

She did as she was told, just as she had as a little girl, reciting the events straight through, as though she were telling the beads of a rosary: this one and this one, until it was done.

She spared him no detail. He sat at the other end of the settle from her and watched the beautiful mouth shape words that described intimacies, perverted acts, brutal deeds. It was impossible to tell if she had distanced herself from what she was saying or didn't care any more. When she had finished, the silence hung between them in the air, heavy with distant violence, past desires. Léon got up, put a taper to the fire, and lit the crasset. He watched the flame flicker toward his fingers and threw it onto the fire at the last moment.

"*Mon Dieu!* How can such a recitation lighten any cross I have to bear?" His voice was hoarse, as if he had been weeping, but she had seen no tears.

The young woman gave a great sigh, as if some cross had been lifted from her instead. "That's better, it's over now." She picked the silver jug up off the hearth and refilled her glass. When she spoke again, her voice was brisk, businesslike.

"I want you to come to Paris with me, while I find a way to get Florian d'Aberville out of France. I need your help to get us back undetected from the coast and onto the island, until I can get him to England. He is very ill, and this is by far the shorter journey by sea. Also, I'm not sure how he would be received in England, and his return would be difficult to keep secret."

Léon was leaning toward the fire as she spoke, and she could sense his reaction in the sudden rigidity of his body, the stillness of his hands. Then he turned to face her. "I've only one question to ask. Why?"

Estelle looked straight into his eyes as she replied, "Because I owe it to him."

"You owe freedom — and risk losing your own — to a drunkard who watched his wife make love with other men, let his wife watch while *he* made love with other men — oh, correction, forgive me — while he made love with your husband. A drunkard who took you by force, against your will? And then, as if this were not enough, connived at your marriage with his pretty boy to get his hands on your fortune?"

The brutality of his words made her feel physically ill, but it also made her angry. "Better by far a man who starts by deceiving you and ends up loving and caring for you, than a man who starts by loving you and ends up deceiving you!"

"Your morality is diabolic. Can this be the girl who shrank from a kiss, a touch on the arm?"

"Oh, yes, Léon. Such naive morality is easily cured by men like you, whose only aim is to strip the petals from such a flower! You might not have raped me, but over the two years of our *fiançailles* — who knows? You are skilled at that game, I gather!"

She was standing up now, facing him, eyes blazing. Her voice shivered deep in her throat. "One day it would be a kiss — 'Just a kiss, Estelle.' That would be granted, for we were engaged, and you were honorable, no? Then it would be a small step to the body pressed closer against mine, the hands around my waist slipping lower, pressing me against you. Then would come the kisses on the neck, the throat — 'just let me just stroke you, Estelle — you're so beautiful. . . . There, isn't that nice? There's no harm, Estelle, and you are making me happy.' Soon it would be the hand on the thigh over the skirt. Then, some lucky afternoon, when parents and guardians have been lulled into a false sense of security, that hand would be under my skirt, and then — and then —"

Léon stood up, shaken out of anger. Was this not what he had thought of before he had looked elsewhere?

"— And then I would feel those fingers against my skin and

be lost, for I have feelings, too — I loved you, and you are handsome!"

Suddenly, she threw herself back against the *lit de fouaille* and pulled her skirts high around her waist, her thighs like mother-of-pearl in the firelight, eyes black with grief and anger. "Not at once would you have taken me, Léon, but little by little, until there would seem no point in not permitting the final *coup de grace.*"

He was close to her now, and she could see he was shaking. "What difference is there, Léon de Polnay, between a man who rapes in two minutes and a man who rapes over two years? Explain that to the ignorant girl who has been fool enough to trust them!"

The tears glittered on her lashes. "Here I am, yours to command! Let me save you time and trouble. In two minutes it can all be over, and I can pretend to be raped, if you prefer it."

He could not. Even as he looked at her thighs, the faint outline of her femaleness against the thin cambric, he was struck down, impotent. "I — —" He seemed to have been struck dumb as well.

"I thought not." In one swift movement Estelle sat up, smoothed her skirt over her legs again. Confused and disoriented, Léon retreated to the settle and sat staring at her.

She continued, in a quiet, sad voice, "You want me a virgin, a flower — and yet you would have me, too. Such a conundrum, is it not? Now that I am spoiled, you don't want me — and yet you would have liked to have taken me, too."

She gasped suddenly and put a hand to her side. "I'm tired, and I shouldn't have become angry. You are no different from other men."

Anger returned the words to him. "Thank you very much. I am wondering if this is really the way to get a man — one whose only fault is to be like other men — back for you."

"I don't know. Is it?" she asked, disconcerting him again.

This time Léon's anger was jolted into laughter, as it so often was at moments of crisis in his life. "Yes, damn you, yes. I'm angry, but your lecture on morality has sufficiently shamed me.

Don't ever become a Sunday-school teacher, Estelle. You would cause chaos and confusion!"

Now that victory appeared to be hers, she looked startled, disoriented. "You'll do it?"

"I'll try. We'll have to do some planning together —" He gave a sudden exclamation. "*Dieu,* it's night now, and I've given no thought as to how you should return."

"I shall stay here. As you said, we have plans to make."

"But, Estelle, your —"

"Reputation?" She gave him the bitter, crooked smile. "I suppose not. And mine is long gone."

The rapprochement began as they smiled at each other. Estelle felt affection now, not the desire that had hit her on the *Nerine* and deprived her of reason. It pleased and saddened her at the same time. "Birds of a feather," she said.

Léon grinned, "True." Above them, the crasset flared up suddenly and the flame burned green for a moment. Léon saw her look up at it and saw the fear come into her eyes. He knew what she was remembering, that the past was indeed back with her, both the evil and the good.

"Those persons of whom one says nothing," she said. "One is close to us."

"Old wives' tales, Estelle. What witch would bother you, here with me?"

She saw a white, waxen face, black eyes, a scarlet gash of mouth. "Oriana."

"Who?" He hadn't caught the name she murmured.

As he leaned forward, she got up from the *lit de fouaille* and came over to him. Like a little child she snuggled against him, this woman who had offered him her body only a few minutes ago. He felt her shake, and he held her tight, as if his strength could drive out from her very bones the presence of terror in the darkness, a corruption beyond the reach of earthly powers.

Chapter Twenty-two

WHEN ESTELLE AWOKE, the sun was well up and she could hear Marie clucking and calling the hens outside. The old woman had left her a nightgown on the bed the night before. Estelle presumed it had belonged to Léon's mother, since it was in his mother's room that Leon had put her. All night Estelle had felt those arms around her, arms whose warmth she had recalled during her journey to le clos de Polnay. Léon had not moved into the large marital bedroom on his mother's death but had retained the smaller room of his childhood.

When Estelle came down the circular stone staircase, she found him sitting at the large table by the window going over some papers. He looked up at her and smiled. "Good morning! You would make a terrible farmer's wife. The sun is well up."

"I'll not argue with that. You haven't changed your mind?" She indicated the mass of papers on the table.

"No, but I'm not a gentleman of leisure, you know. I have things to arrange if I'm to spend time on your affairs." He pulled out the chair beside him. "Sit down. We'll eat and then make a start."

He waited until Marie had served them coffee, fresh rolls, butter and honey, then pushed his papers to one side and began to talk.

"Estelle, you are an island girl, but there are Guernsey ways about which you know nothing. To help you I will have to trust you with secrets few women know. My men will think it unlucky I am taking you into my confidence, let alone allowing you to sail on the *Nerine*. Fortunately, we won't be taking you to Quebec or the Indies, but only as far as Saint-Malo. They won't say no to taking as much money for that as for a trip to the New World."

"You can buy their silence?"

"Yes. They are in it for the adventure *and* the money. They are used to keeping their counsel."

This was a Léon she had not seen before. He was completely serious, and it gave him a withdrawn, cold quality that reminded her somehow of oncle Matthieu. He pushed back his chair and held out his hand to help her up. "They say a picture is worth a thousand words. Come, let me show you."

He led her to a door in the corner of the same room. It looked like a cupboard door, since it was set in an exterior wall. When Léon opened it, it still resembled a closet, for cloaks were hanging on nails around the walls. Leon bent forward and pushed something on the floor.

"It's a trapdoor!"

"Yes. Here, take one of these cloaks. You will need it."

Estelle followed him down solidly constructed wooden steps that went down some distance before she felt a different surface beneath her feet.

"Wait here a moment while I light a lantern."

She stood still in the darkness and heard him take it down from the wall. As the flame rose and strengthened, it illuminated a large cellar that extended well beyond the range of the lantern's light. There was barrels and cases of various kinds around the walls and other objects wrapped in oilskin and ship's canvas.

"No wonder oncle Matthieu was upset when I said you looked the very picture of a smuggler."

His smile gleamed at her in the dim light, pearls from the South Seas in the face of a brigand. "You should see your oncle Matthieu's cellars. The ones in those eighteenth-century Saint Peter Port houses are the very best."

"Oncle Matthieu?"

"Of course! He stays onshore now and tends to the paper-work, but I'm told that in his youth no one could match him."

Estelle looked around. "Is this where we would hide Florian if it were necessary?"

"We could if we needed to. The air is surprisingly dry in our cellars — perfect for the storage and maturing of wines. That's why Guernsey was so prosperous in the great days of privateering. Of course, nowadays the British government in their wisdom have put an end to it. We've been forced underground, you might say."

"It was permitted once?"

"Oh, yes. Your uncle had his letters of marque and could use his boat as a man-of-war. He became very rich — and still is — because he didn't let a little thing like the law stand in his way."

Léon held the lantern high and circled it round the cellar. "We're a bit empty at the moment, because I've been about my lawful business."

"Which is?"

"*Chère* Estelle, to the world — and for much of the time — I'm a merchant with a routine like any clerk at the Royal Court House. I go to Newfoundland for fish, take wine from France to South America, bring sugar or coffee and rum to Quebec, then back to Newfoundland and home again."

"That sounds like a full life, so why do you bother with smuggling?"

The smile gleamed again in the shadows. "Because I have a little larceny in my veins — and to help your poor oncle Matthieu, who can think of no other way to live."

"So straightlaced, proper oncle Matthieu is a criminal!"

"*Nennin!* He's just behind the times. An old fogey!" Léon took her arm again. "This way — we haven't yet finished the tour."

They walked the length of the cellar to a pile of boxes stacked close to the roof. Léon moved them easily, as if they were empty, and Estelle saw they were there for concealment. Behind them lay another door constructed with heavy metal strips of some sort across the wood. Léon pushed back the sturdy bolt and swung it open, holding the lantern high as he did so.

She was looking down a long passageway carved out of the rock itself, with sconces on the walls as if torches were placed there on occasion. There were wheel marks and ruts on the packed earth floor. As Léon closed the door behind them, Estelle felt against her face the colder, damper air of the tunnel in front of them.

"Come." He motioned to her to stay alongside him. "Stay close to the light. The path is slippery in places."

The passage sloped downward as they progressed, with steps cut into the rocks in places. The damp changed to wetness the farther they went. Moisture dripped occasionally from the ceiling, and in places stalactites had formed on the sides. Apart from the occasional drip-drip, there was no sound at all. Even their footsteps were muffled on the moist rock and earth surface below them. At one point, Estelle slipped, and Léon took hold of her elbow.

"It's very wet at the entrance, and we're nearly there," he cautioned.

Suddenly Estelle heard a sound — a murmur, a muffled roar, like the sound in a large pink seashell at Aberville House. "It's the sea!"

Then, without transition, they were blinking in the sunlight, in a small bay with cliffs towering high on three sides. These cliffs were nothing like the bare, precipitous drop of la Rocque Varou but were luxuriantly covered with undergrowth of all kinds. As they emerged from shadow into sun, Estelle could feel the reason. The little cove was incredibly warm, a bowl that caught and held the sun's rays during the hottest part of the day.

"Is this Moulin Huet? If so, I don't remember it."

"No, you've never been here before. It's to the east of Moulin Huet and almost impossible to reach, except by the way we came."

Estelle moved to go forward to the water's edge, but Léon cautioned her, "No, stay back. It's better to stay close to the cliff face during daylight, in case we draw the attention of anyone who might be walking on the cliffs."

Estelle thought of her poet-confessor. Did he come this far, she wondered?

"This is where we shall bring in your cargo," said Leon.

"Can you bring the *Nerine* this far?"

"No, it would attract too much attention. We'll anchor off the coast beyond Jethou. The revenue cutters generally stand off Saint Peter Port or Herm. I have men who can row an eight-oared rowboat straight into the wind's eye and faster than we could get the *Nerine* around the rocks — although I know each one by heart."

Estelle thought of how treacherous the seas could be along these coasts, of an open boat with Florian in it. The difficulty of what she was intending to do was driven home.

"We must pray for fair weather." It was as if he had read her thoughts. "Come, we can safely sit on the rocks over here and feel the sun on our faces."

Estelle lifted her face to the noonday brightness and felt it flow through her like a benediction. "There's some magical salve in the sun," she murmured, as if she were speaking to herself. "I begin to feel whole again."

"Petite étoile."

Estelle opened her eyes and caught an unexpected expression of tenderness on Léon's face. "Your mother used to call me that."

He smiled and turned away from her, changing the subject suddenly. "I'll go into Saint Peter Port this afternoon to work on the *Nerine*. The men will be there, but they'll not be expecting to go anywhere for a while yet. I'll arrange things as quickly as I can. We can get to Paris quite easily, but once there it will be up to you."

"I realize that. I have one possibility to get Florian out, and I pray God he's in Paris to help me."

"A friend of yours?"

"Of Florian's, really. They were at school together. Englishmen seem to stay close to special friends from their schooldays. I suspect he's the only friend Florian has left in Paris, and I'm sure he must be the person responsible for getting Florian out of prison and into hospital."

"Are you sure you don't want to try interceding for him with the French? After all, they freed you, and he is now ill."

Estelle shook her head. "I can't risk it. The way things are at the moment, I don't think he would be welcome in England, and I myself might be in jeopardy in both countries. There'll be no Eugénie to intercede for me now — she's rarely in Paris at this time, and I think it is to her, in part, that I owe my freedom."

Léon stood up and held out his hand. "We'd better go back now. It's a steep climb up the cliff, but it will prepare you for what lies ahead."

In fact, Estelle felt less tired than she had the day before, and realized her strength was returning. Seated across from her in the big parlour, Léon nodded approvingly.

"Good, you're not as weak as I feared. Do you want me to take you back to Le Refuge to make arrangements?"

Estelle shook her head. "I think not. I would be grateful if you would tell them I am safe and well, and staying here for the time being. My uncle may be quite happy to smuggle brandy but he would never consent to what I intend to do. Even before my memory returned, I could see in their eyes what they felt about my past. That I should be planning to bring part of it here would arouse their deepest opposition." Out of nowhere came a spirit of gaiety, lightening her heart. "Oh, Léon, I'm already such a lost soul! Could it make matters any worse if they believe that I'm your mistress?"

He seemed to have been infected by the same mood. Suddenly he swung her around and held her against him, laughing down into her face. "Then why don't we make it true? I promise not to care any more that you are a flower stripped of its petals. I promise to reform, to make love to you with the keenest enthusiasm, the greatest skill, the most passionate ardor —" In between each phrase he kissed her gently on the ear, the nose, the forehead. As he bent to her mouth, she put her hand on his chest and pushed him away from her.

"Ta-ta-ta, monsieur! Such speed, such rapidity for a two-year seducer! Those kisses will more than suffice for a week or so. If you are reformed, then so am I, Léon de Polnay. It will take two years for you to make love to me."

They were both of them laughing, breathless, excited. A dangerous game, she thought, a dangerous game. It must stop here, before the skinny little boy who had fought her battles was eclipsed by this impossibly handsome pirate who, she had determined, was to rescue her imprisoned lover. She must not weaken.

Before dusk that evening, Léon left for Saint Peter Port with a letter for oncle Matthieu and a list for Celestine of clothes and belongings that Estelle required. Estelle stood in the doorway and smiled up at him, and he thought how well she seemed to belong beneath the great arch.

As Estelle handed over the list, Léon grumbled, "an errand-boy for you, that's what I am. How did such a thing come to pass, I ask myself?"

"Because you are bored, Léon."

"I am an errand-boy because I am bored?" he exclaimed in mock outrage.

"You remind me of — someone else I know, who fled from boredom as though it were the plague. You're tired of being a good little merchant-boy, for the time being, and that's why you're an errand-boy."

Unaccountably, he looked saddened by her remark. "If you say so, Estelle, you're probably right. I'll be back tomorrow. *A bientôt.*" He swung his horse around and was off down the winding pathway to the road beyond.

For the next twenty-four hours, Estelle and Marie turned out the house in a flurry of spring cleaning. Although Marie was still uncommunicative, she was glad to have the young girl's company. Together they worked methodically through parlors, storerooms, larders, linen cupboards.

The house bore evidence of the solid prosperity of the de Polnay family in the good mahogany furniture made by the Guilles in Pedvin Street, the fine Turkish carpets, the mirrors with heavily ornate frames. From the condition of the linens and curtains Estelle could see that a woman's touch had long been absent. Although of fine quality, signs of wear and tear were evident, and there was much that needed replacing. Marie had obviously laundered, starched, and ironed assiduously but had not taken it upon herself to go further.

That night, as the old servant handed Estelle the lamp to take up to her room, she pointed at the parlor window. Above the trees, Estelle could see the moon ringed in clouds. "*Cherne à la lune, le vent, la pluie, ou la brume,*" Marie intoned sonorously.

"So the circle around the moon means bad weather?"

"*Ouai.* Wind, fog, rain — something bad."

"Better soon than later," murmured Estelle. As if anxious not to overhear anything Estelle might have to keep secret, the old woman moved swiftly away toward the shadows of the kitchen.

Chapter Twenty-three

LÉON RETURNED almost exactly twenty-four hours after his departure. He strode into the house and straight through to where Estelle was sitting in the parlor.

"Get your cloak, Estelle. All is arranged."

"What —"

"Don't look so astounded! When I move, I move quickly."

"Where are my clothes and my belongings?"

"Safely on board the *Nerine*."

"The men have agreed?"

"Yes. Smuggling a man is little different to them than smuggling an anker-full of brandy, as long as they are paid. It doesn't go against their principles."

"What about my presence?"

"There were some superstitious mutterings, but the trap was already baited. The gathering dusk suits us well. I want to draw as little attention as possible to you from now on."

A few minutes later, they got into an open carriage and headed back to Saint Peter Port.

"Pull your hood up around your face," Léon counseled her

"But don't appear too secretive or nervous if we meet anyone. My neighbors are not unused to seeing me with a pretty woman." He smiled at her and turned his attention to the road again.

It was dark when the carriage rattled through the streets of Saint Peter Port harbor. A light rain was falling and the wind started to rise.

"What will you do with the horse and carriage?" Estelle asked.

"What I usually do. Marie's brother will take it back to Saint Martin's tomorrow with provisions for his sister and then keep it for me until I need it again."

As they reached the open esplanade, the wind grew stronger, and Estelle could hear the comparatively calm waters of the inner harbor slapping vigorously against the supporting wall. The now-familiar outline of the *Nerine* was visible among the lights from the smaller boats. Léon brought the horses to a standstill in the area where Maturin l'Eustace had kept his cart and pulled out his watch.

"Good, just as I hoped. I told Marie's brother to come about an hour from now because I didn't want us to meet." He tied up both horse and carriage securely, and they were off through the darkness. "The dinghy is moored at the foot of the steps over there. It will take us out to the *Nerine*."

This time, in the dark and rain, the steps down the side of the harbor wall were far more difficult, but the night and the weather provided perfect cover. Léon untied the boat from its moorings and looked up at the sky. "What we smugglers call 'the darks'," he muttered. He gave her a wink she could just make out through the gloom and started to row strongly toward the cutter, the dinghy dipping and bobbing alarmingly over the whitecaps that been whipped up on the water's surface. As they reached the side of the *Nerine*, Léon called out, "*Wharro, Pierre, mon viow!*"

High above them on the cutter's deck appeared the head of the crewman Estelle remembered from her first visit. "You made it, eh?" Pierre disappeared again, and there was a rattling sound as the rope ladder came down the side of the *Nerine,* splashing into the water beside them.

"The *Nerine* will dip and sway," cautioned Léon, "so hold fast, move slowly, and stop if there's a sudden heavy swell. Move with the ladder — I'll be behind you."

Estelle stood up and held the edge of the dinghy, then transferred her hands to the rope. For a moment she felt panic. "*Chut!*" she thought. "Can I face asking him to row me back to Le Refuge and oncle Matthieu?"

The rope ladder suddenly seemed almost welcoming. Without further hesitation she started to climb, hand over hand, slowly and steadily. She felt the movement of the ladder behind her as Léon began his ascent. The cutter suddenly lurched away from them, and the ladder flopped sickeningly against it, disappearing beneath her. She gasped as her feet slipped on the rungs and then felt Léon's hand holding her ankle.

"Nearly there. You're all right now." He sounded calm, unconcerned. From above, the face and hands of Pierre emerged from the darkness.

"Give me your hand as you reach the rail, madame." She did so and felt herself hauled over the side, to land in an undignified heap at the seaman's feet. A moment later, Léon appeared.

"You did well," he said approvingly. "The last time this *fainéant* did that in a storm he fell off into the harbor."

Pierre looked hurt. "Yes, but that was different. I was drunk," he said with dignity. He touched his seaman's cap at Estelle. "Good night, madame." He gave her a look that was by no means welcoming and left them.

"We'll follow his example. It's getting bad up here now." Below decks, the pitching seemed even heavier than it had on the open deck.

"I hope you don't suffer from seasickness. This promises to be a rough crossing."

Estelle thought of her first departure from Saint Peter Port, sitting on the deck of the steamer wrapped in oilskins and crying because of the man who now stood beside her. "I think not," she replied. "When do we leave?"

"Very soon. Although we don't need the cover of night, I see no point in wasting time. I've plenty of places to hide our secret cargo when we return."

Estelle looked around at the compact, austere space below decks. "Where would you have a hiding place on this ship?' she asked.

"You ask that of a smuggler, dear lady? Where do I *not* have a hiding place! Let me show you."

He knelt on the floor and put his hands on the planking, tapping the timbers one after the other. Estelle noticed that one of them made a different sound. "It's hollow," she said.

"Yes, it's really a chest. We used to fill it with tea. And over there—" he pointed at some ballast bags standing in a corner "—those bags can be hollowed out, or you can pack silk goods in bales to look like the real thing. I've even seen silk carried in a hollowed-out ham!"

He told her of keels and yards that carried spirits, of tobacco twisted into ropes inside hawsers and packed among a raft of timbers to look like log-ends. "But," he added, "I would never dream of hiding your English aristo in a hempen rope. Follow me, madame."

His cabin was as she remembered it, but when he lit the lamp she saw a small pile of her belongings on his bunk.

"You and your aristo will use this. If there's an emergency, we'll put him in here." At the head of the bunk, Léon removed a couple of wooden plugs from what looked like planking. Underneath were screws that loosened easily and came out to allow the boards to pull open. The "wall" was actually a sizable closet, stretching back into the ship's side, big enough to hold a man.

"Not luxury, but there's enough air and it's dry. I don't think we'll need it, but at least you know it's here."

Beneath her feet, Estelle sensed a change in the movement of the ship. "Are we on our way?"

"As I said, no need to waste any time. We'll stay here in case the Revenue cutters are on the prowl, until we clear Herm and Jethou."

A few minutes later, the movement of the *Nerine* changed again, as they encountered the full force of the gale in the channel between the islands. The creaking of the rigging and the groaning of the ship's planking rose to new crescendos, and Estelle could hear the ship's crew calling to each other on deck.

"Dieu!" Léon looked concerned. "The way the wind is blowing, we'll be past the Little Russel and into the Grand Russel in no time." He got off the sea-chest on which he had been sitting, opened it, and pulled out some oilskins. "Here, put these on. I must check and see how things are going with the men."

As they emerged through the hatchway onto the foredeck, the howling wind hurled rain and spray into their faces. Estelle tasted salt on her lips. Over the noise of wind and waters Léon shouted back at her, "When you get on deck, keep hold of the ropes slung around the deck. Never let go of them, do you understand?"

She nodded, blinking the stinging spray out of her eyes. Through it she could see Pierre at the ship's wheel, shouting at some men working on the ship's rigging.

"Stay here while I talk to them." Léon grabbed hold of a rope near him, and she watched as he worked his way around to his second-in-command. As he got there, one of the men jumped from the shrouds and began to speak urgently to him. He was using patois, but there was no mistaking the anger and hostility in his tone. From the occasional word that drifted her way Estelle knew she was the topic of conversation. She reached out for one of the ropes slung at the side of the ship, and was flung against the foot of the rigging. Grasping the soaked wood beneath her hands, she wound her fingers through the rope attached to it. In front of her, the horizon tilted crazily and then righted itself briefly again. Between sheets of driving rain, she caught a glimpse of Herm and Jethou in the distance. There was no sign of Guernsey any more.

"Get below! You must stay below!" Léon's body cannoned into her, driving her against the rigging.

"No! I'm not afraid!"

"They are!" He was holding her by the shoulder and pointing toward the crewmen in the rigging. He pushed her toward the hatchway, down the steps, and into the belly of the cutter once more. In the cabin, water pouring from their oilskins, they faced each other.

"You cannot go up until we reach safe harbor. They say you are a witch."

She saw the anger in his eyes and wondered how much was hostility and how much was his own unadmitted fear. He was an islander himself, steeped in the superstition of generation upon generation who believed in fairies and sorceresses and their power to harm. She felt a powerful wave of fright within herself as the cutter lurched wildly beneath their feet, and it made her challenge him to cover her own weakness.

"And you, Léon de Polnay? Do you think I have the power to bring about tempests, cause the winds to shriek, and the waters to roar? Do you — *do you?*"

The fear was still there when he faced her, his eyes meeting hers briefly and turning away. "You made me do this, didn't you? Am I a madman, that I ignore storm warnings and set out on an expedition to bring your lover back to Guernsey, to my own home? My mother must be spinning in her grave! What else can it be but that I am bewitched — tell me that!"

Léon didn't wait to be told. As the final word left him, he spun on his heel and walked out, slamming the cabin door behind him.

Carefully, Estelle removed her soaking oilskins and shoes, turned back the coverlet on the bunk, and laid her head on the round, hard bolster. Her feet suddenly swung higher than her head, and then the cabin righted itself again.

As if to convince herself — or some listening spirit — she said out loud to the cabin walls, "I'm no witch. I am the victim of a witch."

As the sound of her voice blended with the straining and

creaking of every rope and plank around her, Estelle was struck by the irony of what she had said. Her own belief in the power of another being to enchant, to subvert and to destroy was as strong as that of any of the men now fighting the elements she was believed to hold in her thrall.

Chapter Twenty-four

IT WAS THE CALM that woke Estelle. Beneath her, the *Nerine* rocked gently, at rest in safe harbor. She could hear the now-familiar noises of the cutter around her and the harsh crying of the gulls. Faintly, from somewhere in the distant past, came the words of a lullaby.

Papa a dit qui fallait dormir,
Lo, lo, lo, le p'tit,
Pis qu'papa a dit,
Faudra dormir.

"Papa said you must go to sleep, little one." Who had sung that to her? Probably Celestine, the only mother figure Estelle had known. No, not quite true, for there had also been Léon's mother. Would she ever have children of her own, Estelle wondered, to hold in her arms and sing to? Or any semblance of a normal life, for that matter? It seemed very unlikely such a thing would ever come to pass.

She put on the fresh clothes Celestine had packed for her,

brushed out her hair, pinned it up, and let herself out of the cabin with her small bag of possessions.

No one was around on deck, and Estelle presumed they were all sleeping after a night of fighting the storm. Surveying Saint-Malo, which lay in a clear, watery morning sunlight, she went over her plan of action in her mind. First, she must get herself to Paris by train. Once there, everything else hinged on Albert Jolivet, the only friend Estelle had met who was primarily part of Florian's cultural and intellectual life. It was Albert Jolivet who had acquired for Florian the Canova statues at Bostock Hall, as well as some of the finer objets d'art at Aberville House. He was an antiquarian of French and English extraction, now living mainly in Paris, on the Boulevard des Capucines. Their friendship dated from Eton, where Albert, a bewildered boy who spoke barely a word of English, had found himself protected by Florian d'Aberville. He had never forgotten, and Estelle knew she could count on him, if he were there. Her name would cause problems if she had to draw attention to herself by asking for help elsewhere. But she would face that problem if it arose, and not before.

"Good morning." Estelle started at the greeting and turned to face Léon, who was standing at the entrance to the hatchway. From his gray face she saw that what sleep he had managed had been of short duration.

"Good morning. I have put together the things I need and will leave you now. If things go as I plan in Paris, I will be returning in a day or two. If things take too long and you have to leave, I will take rooms here somewhere and wait for you to return. Florian, of course, will have no passport, or I would discharge you of your responsibility at this point."

Léon looked as if he were having difficulty taking in what she was saying. "Hold your horses, Estelle. I'll need a little time to gather my things together."

"I'm going on my own. I've decided it would be better. I'll not attract as much attention as you would in Paris — you look far more like a conspirator than I do. If necessary, I can get an attendant to help me with Florian."

Léon didn't attempt to argue with Estelle. His own exhaustion and his responsibility for the *Nerine* and its crew were uppermost in his mind.

"Agreed." His voice was as unemotional as hers had been. "Unless it becomes imperative, I will be here. Most of the men have family or *petites amies* here in Saint-Malo, and the offer of a paid holiday is not to be sneezed at."

"How would you prefer me to let you know when I return? It would be better not just to arrive with Florian at the *Nerine*."

"Go to the Hôtel du Bon Chemin in the Rue Lafitte. The rooms are cheap and clean; the proprietor is discreet and knows me. You can get a message to me from there."

"Thank you." There didn't seem much else to say.

"C'est rien. Bonne chance, Estelle."

"Good luck? A strange thing to wish a witch, isn't it? I'm glad you all survived my best efforts last night."

Léon shrugged his shoulders and made an attempt at a laugh. Now that the storm was over, he was embarrassed at the memory of his superstitious fear.

She didn't really judge him at all. She knew only too well the terror that can strike the soul at the power of another to charm.

It was a particularly trying journey from Saint-Malo to Paris for one used to traveling *en grand luxe* in the private splendors of the emperor's own train. At the onset of the journey, Estelle produced from her reticule a small bible she had found on the bedside table at le clos de Polnay. Any possible misconceptions about her solitary state were avoided by the nature of her reading matter, as was the possibility of being drawn into conversation.

On arrival at the Gare du Nord, she took a fiacre straight to the Boulevard des Capucines. To her relief, the concierge informed her that Monsieur Jolivet was indeed in his rooms. The antiquarian was astounded to see her, but shook her hand warmly, tears in his eyes.

"I cannot believe it is you, Principessa! I'd even thought of trying to write to you, but I was afraid of drawing attention to myself. I don't know if the emperor cares about my efforts for Florian at all, but I have been of more use to our poor friend by staying in the background, I'm sure."

"Where is he, monsieur Jolivet?"

"In the Hôpital des petites soeurs de Marie. I have managed to persuade the authorities to keep him there."

As they ate some supper together, Estelle described her plans to him. "Is it possible that the staff can be bribed, so that I can remove him from the hospital?"

Albert Jolivet smiled ruefully at her. "Unlikely, *chère madame*. The hospital is run by an order of nuns." At her crestfallen expression, he added, "But don't worry. There is a way, because I've already thought of doing it myself. The problem for me was how to get him out of France, and you have taken care of that. Since the weather has turned warm, they have allowed me to wheel him into the gardens for an hour or two in the afternoon. The convent attached to the hospital is not a closed order, and there is no guard on the gate. If one had a carriage outside, one could simply leave."

"Wonderful! Let's do it as soon as possible. But you must be certain to go and speak to an attendant while I take Florian. I can leave the country, Monsieur Jolivet. You cannot. If you could arrange for a carriage and a driver prepared to help with an invalid as far as the coast, I would be very grateful."

From a pouch concealed in the skirt of her dress, Estelle produced a pearl-and-diamond necklace Florian had given her. Some of her possessions had found their way out of France with her, and she could only presume that her maid had given them to oncle Matthieu. Many had disappeared.

"I would like to keep such money as I have for our journey back. Perhaps you could use the proceeds from this to hire the carriage and driver." Estelle knew that Albert Jolivet's ambassador father had squandered most of the family fortune and that he now lived chiefly by his antiquarian skills. Jolivet took the money with unconcealed gratitude, saying, "I'm in no position to refuse, madame. I must admit that Florian's illness has already cost me much."

"I imagine it has," said Estelle. "I hope it will be possible for me to stay here tonight? Every respectable hotel in Paris keeps a register, and I wish to attract as little attention as possible."

Albert Jolivet smiled wryly. "That would be in my best interests as well, Principessa."

She spent an uneasy, restless night. It was a relief to see the dawn and to hear her host up and about. By the time she had dressed, he had already gone out to put their plans in motion.

Albert Jolivet returned about midday, jubilant. A carriage and driver would be waiting for a young woman and an invalid that afternoon at about three o'clock, outside the hospital. The driver was prepared to go on right through the night, if necessary to Saint-Malo, and he had asked few questions. The money Jolivet had offered was more than the man could have hoped to earn in two weeks, and he had a family to support. Jolivet had also supplied provisions for the journey.

By two-thirty, they were at the Hôpital des petites soeurs de Marie, walking along the corridors with bare, white-washed walls and into the ward, along rows of narrow beds.

Florian was terribly, horribly changed. Estelle had known he must be but had not imagined such a remnant of a man. Was there any flesh left at all, or was this merely his skeleton she would take back to Le Refuge, to rattle about her closeted room until death took him?

She had expected to feel affection, grief, even pity. She had not expected to feel revulsion. She staggered, weak with shock at his appearance, and felt her frozen mouth stretch into a smile. "Florian — it's Estelle."

"Estelle." An emaciated hand crept over the thin coverlet and reached for hers. "I . . . don't . . . believe it."

"Believe it — it's me." She took the long, brittle fingers in hers and bent closer over the gaunt figure.

"Star-lady." His voice was like dead leaves rustling.

"Yes. Will we go out into the garden?"

"No — stay here. Happy with you."

Despairingly, she looked up at Albert Jolivet.

"Of course we'll go out, my friend. It's more cheerful outside, for Estelle as well as for you." The antiquarian hurried over to a nun who was passing.

Estelle knelt down beside Florian, whose eyes followed her every movement. "Florian, I've come to take you away. There's nothing for you to do or to worry about. Just trust me."

"Always."

She was relieved to see that he could sit up and get into the bath-chair, although with great difficulty. She hardly found it possible to believe he could have changed so much in only four months. As they manoeuvered the chair onto a sunlit terrace above sloping lawns, she whispered to Albert Jolivet, "Why such a fast deterioration?"

"They say he has no will to live." Albert Jolivet pointed at an entrance gate at the bottom of the lawn. *"Là-bas,"* he said quietly. "That one. Continue walking with him when I get the chair onto the path there. I will go and speak to the nun by the long windows over there, to take her attention. May good fortune smile on you, Principessa."

"And you, monsieur Jolivet. Thank you for all your kindness." They started to walk toward the path.

"God go with you." For a moment he stood with his hand on Florian's shoulder, and theh he was gone.

Accelerating her steps, Estelle walked along the path and beyond the arch of the entrance gate. The carriage that Jolivet had described to her was waiting beneath the arch of trees in the shade. The driver, a sturdy-looking man in his forties, jumped down as she approached. "What do we do with the chair, madame?" he asked without preamble.

"We leave it here, outside the wall — if you could help monsieur into the carriage."

The driver picked Florian up as though he were a small child, and Estelle pushed the chair against the wall. Moments later, they were on their way.

They didn't stop again until night had fallen, but Estelle was so concerned at Florian's condition that she decided to risk staying at a coaching inn. At dawn, they were on their way once more. Her name had aroused neither questions nor suspicion from the innkeeper, but it was as if a great weight had been lifted from her when she saw the outskirts of Saint-Malo ahead of them the next day.

On the seat opposite her, Florian lay — in sleep or coma, she couldn't be sure. Looking on this man who seemed more dead than alive, she wondered what in heaven's name she had done, and why. Apart from his initial reaction, he seemed unaware of her presence or the fact that he was being set free. His breathing was so light that at times she wondered if he were dead, and she frequently leaned over him to feel the faint whisp of his breath on her cheek.

At Saint-Malo, the driver found the Rue Lafitte and helped her get Florian into the Hôtel du Bon Chemin before he left. She wished him a safe return to Paris and watched him go with a further feeling of release. Another link with the capital had gone. Now all that remained was to get a message to Léon de Polnay. The hotel proprietor's manner reminded Estelle of Marie. He showed a distinct lack of curiosity about what was going on around him and agreed to send her message without asking any questions.

Just as she had done on the Boulevard des Capucines, she sat down and waited. Beside her, on the bed, Florian lay and slept. About an hour later after they had arrived, he opened his eyes and looked at her. To her surprise, she caught a gleam of intelligence and interest in his look, something to suggest that there was still a thinking being within this hollow carapace of a man.

"You came back for me." The voice was recognizable for the first time, not just a rasping sound devoid of personality and masculinity.

"As soon as I could. I have been ill, but as soon as I was recovered, I came for you."

"Perhaps I will live now."

"Of course, you will. You have me now, Florian, so you will live."

The door opened. Léon stood there, in his seaman's boots,

his heavy Guernsey sweater, the gold earring glistening beneath the dark hair. His vitality seemed to reverberate against the walls of the small room and Estelle felt herself drained by its power.

"You are a miracle worker," said Léon. "I never thought you would be back so soon."

He strode toward the bed, hand extended, obviously determined to be the courteous, correct gentleman. At the sight of Florian, he stopped abruptly, unable for a moment to conceal his reaction of shock. Estelle saw him clench his fists, then smile with a fixedness she recognized from her own reaction in Paris. When he spoke, his voice was clipped, unemotional.

"M'sieu, I would like to get you on board tonight, if you can make it."

"With Estelle here, there's nothing I cannot do."

Léon gave a stiff little bow. "I will have a carriage here in ten minutes, Estelle," he said. "Be ready."

Estelle was still facing the door through which he had gone when she felt the cold, thin hand creeping over hers again.

"Estelle. Star-lady." When she turned to Florian, she saw his eyes were anguished, pleading. "Is he your lover, Estelle? Your husband?"

Estelle turned briefly back to the door, as if to revive herself with the lingering vitality of Léon's presence, to forget the memento mori that lay before her.

"He is neither."

"I cannot believe it."

From her pocket, Estelle took out the little bible and put her hand upon it. "Florian, I swear to you that you were — and still are — the only one who has been both to me. My husband and my lover."

His hand joined hers as she swore her oath of adultery and deceit on that most holy of books, as she felt the corruption of the past seeping back into present, to haunt her again with its memories.

Chapter Twenty-five

THE NIGHT WAS AS BLACK and soft as velvet, as calm as if a benediction had soothed the elements. Heaven, earth, and ocean lay silent in the early evening, unmoved this time by Estelle's presence on the *Nerine*. The crew had helped Florian on board, playing the role of friends helping a drunken companion. One of the port officials had come onto the *Nerine* earlier, but he seemed more concerned with hidden cargo than with human beings. He had checked the crew's papers, and the crew had brought Florian onto the ship afterward. It was also evident that the official was a good friend of Léon de Polnay's.

Now Florian lay on Léon's bunk, sleeping like a child, his breathing seeming less fragile than it had previously. He had even had something to eat and drink, and asked where they were going.

"To Guernsey."

"So much the better." He seemed relieved at the news, and then he had fallen asleep. Estelle put blankets from the sea-chest on the floor and took what rest she could. When she saw the first pale streaks in the night sky through the porthole, she risked leaving him and going up on deck.

Only Pierre Gosselin and one other man were about when she came up. They seemed undisturbed this time by her presence and went on with what they were doing. Estelle turned toward the islands.

"The Islands of the Blest." It was Léon, warmly wrapped against the chill morning air, his eyes fixed on the horizon. "Men have called them by that name from early times. When you see them at this hour or against the setting sun, you understand why."

Looking back afterward, it would seem to Estelle that at this moment she fell in love with Léon de Polnay — for the first time, the second time, the only time. . . . Who knew? It came to her as if carried on the salt sea breeze, without touch or even a glance from those mesmerizing amber eyes that looked toward their island.

Estelle already knew his touch could make the blood race in her veins, that his glance could melt both reason and resolution, but now she caught a glimpse of his soul and she loved him for it. And at this moment, of all moments, all she could say was, "Yes, I do. They seem beautiful to me. I long to see Saint Peter Port again."

"We'll not be coming in at the harbor. You, I, and the gentleman will be leaving the *Nerine* quite shortly."

Before she could ask anything more, a light flickered in the direction of Jethou. Léon left her side and joined Pierre Gosselin at the wheel. A moment later, she saw him near the bowsprit, a lantern in his hand. She watched as one lamp answered the other across the lightening darkness, the *faëu boulanger* of this smuggler's world.

Quietly, she went and stood by his side. "What would you do if it were daylight? Would you have had to risk going in?"

"No, we would have used the sail for signalling. No need now — all is well."

They were making for Jethou, the tiny island close to Herm, little more than a large precipitous rock. Gradually, out of the morning mist, a small jetty came into view. Léon turned to Estelle. "Go down and put all your belongings together, and wake him. Two of the men will come down to you when it is time."

Estelle took one more look at the wild, rocky coastline the *Nerine* would have to negotiate and made her way down to the cabin where Florian lay sleeping.

After about an hour Pierre and another man came down for them. Estelle knew they had already reached the jetty, because she felt the light bump as the *Nerine* touched the side. Pierre Gosselin gave her some instructions.

"Take your belongings, madame. Leave nothing here. When we get on deck do not speak or make any noise."

A plank had been laid between the *Nerine* and the jetty. Pierre, sure-footed as a cat despite his well-padded figure, carried Florian over. Before Estelle had time to consider the width of the plank, the other man had taken her by the arm and pushed her firmly across.

Jethou looked utterly deserted, apart from the gulls that shrieked and dipped overhead. Behind her, she heard Léon giving instructions to the crew who were remaining on board and watched Pierre run back across the makeshift gangway to join them. The other man now supported Florian and was half carrying him to the end of the jetty.

There was a sound on the shingle below, and a large rowboat moved out from the shadows, scraping over the stony beach. The three men in it had obviously done this many times before, moving with patterned precision through a well-rehearsed drama.

Silently, swiftly, the boat with its cargo moved out into the Little Russel, propelled by its great oars padded with canvas and spun yarn. It was heading toward the southwest, away from the harbor of Saint Peter Port.

They had been fortunate indeed with the weather, for even in these conditions, it was a distance to row. On this side of the island the cliffs towered high above them, without sign of human habitation. On the west side they could easily have been seen from the low-lying stretches of Cobo and Vazon Bay, with the coast roads running behind them.

Suddenly, above her, Estelle saw the great shape of la Rocque Varou, bright in the slanting rays of the rising sun. Two of the men broke from their rowing to touch charms around their necks and mutter under their breath, just as Maturin l'Eustace had done to la Gran'mère du Chimquière.

The oarsmen obviously knew the route well. They slackened their speed somewhat as they passed la Rocque Varou but picked up the pace again as they approached Fermain Bay. It was the point at which they were most likely to be seen, and they did not relax until they approached Saint Martin's Point.

There were groans of relief as they rounded it and slowed their pace once more.

On the south coast, the appearance of the cliff face changed, with the heavier cover of vegetation Estelle remembered from the secret cove. There was another murmur from the men as the small sandy beach came into sight around a jutting line of rocks.

"La v'la. Dieu merci!"

They brought the boat in swiftly, running onto the shingle and jumping out as soon as it touched the shore. The most powerfully built of the men picked Florian up in his arms and ran up the beach toward the cave entrance. Estelle wouldn't have known it was there if she hadn't seen it before. As the other men hauled the boat up the beach and under cover, Léon took Estelle's arm and ran with her toward the passage entrance, pulling her along as her shoes slipped on the damp sand.

"Quick! It's far too bright for my liking, and the men are nervous."

In the darkness of the tunnel, Estelle felt panic. "Where's Florian?"

"Probably already in the cellar. I had a litter here by the entrance, so that they could carry him up more easily."

In the moment before Léon lit the lamp for them, Estelle

touched his arm. She could hear his breathing, still heavy from the exertion of rowing, feel the muscle beneath the damp shirt.

"How can I thank your men?"

"By disappearing from their lives as quickly as possible and never reappearing. Oh — and by keeping your counsel, of course."

There was silence for a moment. Then she heard him give a little laugh, but he said nothing more.

"Thank you, Léon." Estelle could not trust herself to say more. More was dangerous; more could show him what she had discovered for herself on the deck of the *Nerine,* as they had watched the islands appear out of the mist.

"No questions as to how you might thank me, Estelle? Two words are enough for me, you think?"

She could hear the pain and hurt in his voice. Estelle closed her eyes, felt the tears pricking behind her eyelids.

"No, but I can think of nothing else." More lies, she thought. How good I have become at deception! In the darkness, she felt his hands on her shoulders turning her toward him.

"I can," he whispered. "I can."

Léon pulled her against him and she felt his lips against her own. He tasted of sea salt and salt sweat and the perfume of the *Nerine* that she now knew so well — pine-tar, okum, tobacco. She could hear their breathing, the surf on the shingle beyond the cave, the blood pounding in her head.

This was how it should have been, all those years ago . . . before Florian, Cosi, and Oriana. It should have been her and this pirate, this explosion of feeling that made her legs shake under her, her hands fumble for the edge of his jacket to clutch at his shirt, feel his body against her fingertips.

But she now knew it was more than this. It was the dawning of a feeling that lay beyond her experience, beyond eroticism or the maternal instinct that had attached her as much as any other instinct to Florian. She had fallen in love with this man: with his good looks, his vitality, his humor, his courage, his soul.

And it was too late. With the onrush of memory's return she had thrown herself into resuscitating part of her past, and she could no longer make any sense of why she had done it.

"I can't, Léon."

"I don't intend that you should." For a moment, they faced each other in the darkness. Then Léon took down one of the torches from the wall and lit it. As the flame flared up, each could see the other's startled, longing face.

"I only intend that you should have some regrets for what might have been, just as I have for what I did so long ago. At this moment in our lives, Estelle, I can think of nothing else we could possibly share. Come."

He took her by the hand and led her up the inside of the cliff to where Florian was waiting for her, to the future she had chosen.

Chapter Twenty-six

WHEN THE LIGHT SHONE on Jethou now, Estelle knew what it was. No will-o'-the-wisp, no fairy gold, but a shaft of light from a dark lantern, a flash from a Congreve match, a needle to pierce her heart. When the gun was fired on Castle Cornet to start the day, she would go and look out at the harbor, at the cutters and luggers, the schooners and merchantmen. If the *Nerine* was there, Estelle felt pain and delight. If it wasn't there, neither was the delight.

Beneath the fig tree, within the espaliered walls of Le Refuge, *la belle veuve* tended her lover as the hot summer sun ripened the fruit and brought forth an overflowing harvest for the island. "Beautiful widow" was what they called her in Saint Peter Port, and she was doubly so. Her husband who had never made love to her was dead, and her lover was now lover in name only.

"Do you love me, Estelle?"

"I love you, Florian."

He was satisfied with words, and so was she. Estelle never wanted him to touch her again. Her mind and body cried out for someone else, and she allowed it to do so, never stopping the thoughts that tore at her sleeping and waking hours. Self-flagellation, a hair-shirt worn in memory of past sins, the deep dungeon of her own mistakes.

Oncle Matthieu and tante Colinette had removed themselves and their children from any contact with her. That was about the limit of their outrage, for the dower wing was hers, as was what was left of her fortune. Besides, oncle Matthieu now had to pray nightly (to a God who, he believed, understood his smuggling ways) that tolerance would ensure Estelle's silence.

Celestine loved Florian. The old servant's principles shifted abruptly when she saw that she was needed again as "nou-nou" by someone as helpless and in need of nursing as "this poor man who is *very* sick." No constable came to ask questions or disturb them, for Celestine's stories of Estelle's pious devotion and the saintly stoicism of the hapless sufferer bore no relationship to any rumors of political assassination or moral corruption.

During the month of June, Florian seemed to improve steadily. He stopped hallucinating and suffering from nightmares and began to regain an appetite. He started to take an interest in his surroundings, although he showed a positive aversion to leaving the walls of Le Refuge. Celestine approved completely, for Florian was fast becoming the perfect small child she had once had in Estelle.

All Florian wanted was to sit and read about the island and its customs. He had even started to learn some of the patois from old Luc, who found this a source of great amusement. Other than that, Florian liked to have Estelle by his side as she embroidered and knitted, having taken up once again the old skills of her childhood. Celestine would look at them together, nodding her approval at this child-man and child-woman playing at house, with no trouble-making passion to disturb the harmony.

Estelle didn't mind the endless hours of sitting and watching herself being watched by both Florian and Celestine. She listened patiently as Celestine rambled on about illness and fate, how all was for the best. She could bear the razor in her ribs when she saw the *Nerine*, or when she saw it wasn't there.

All that she could endure. What gave her cause for anxiety was the growing awareness of a new element in Florian's role as spectator. Day by day, a disturbing nuance crept into their conversation and made its presence felt in the silences that lay between sentences, in the intonation of a word or phrase.

Florian did not trust her. As the remarks gradually built up into a picture, Estelle realized to her horror that he seemed to think she was living another life while he slept or rested.

"Where were you this morning, my love?"

"I went into town, to the shoemaker."

"Ah, I see. Was Celestine with you?"

"You know she wasn't, Florian. She was here with you."

"Of course, silly of me. I thought I heard you talking to someone."

"Where?"

"Outside the wall, when you came back."

"I spoke to no one."

"Must have been my imagination." Silence for a few moments, as he ostensibly returned to his book.

"D'you see that feller — you know, the one whose boat we came on?"

"Never."

"Never, eh? That's strange, small place like this. You sure you never see him . . . in town, I mean?"

"Quite sure." The silence would lie between them again and Estelle would clench her fists, knowing that the matter wasn't yet over.

"Handsome man . . . saw the way he looked at you. You'd like him, Estelle. That is, if you haven't already —"

"Dear God, Florian, why won't you believe me? I want no one! If you don't believe me, come with me next time I leave Le Refuge."

"No, no, no!"

It was then she felt afraid as she watched him shake. It was not his suspicions that gave her the most fear, but his tenuous hold on sanity. His body seemed to be getting stronger, but his mind appeared permanently altered.

For a few days after one of these episodes he would appear content once more, and she would think she had exaggerated its significance. Then it would happen again. It seemed to her that the intervals between were growing shorter, and she decided to speak to Celestine about it. The old woman's response was much as it had been when she had gone to her as a child with her doubts. She had ridiculed her gently, hugged her warmly, and then sent her on her way.

Maybe I am imagining it, Estelle thought. Maybe it's my own sanity I should be questioning. A burning longing filled her to be in contact with someone, anyone outside her own cloistered world, apart from shopkeepers and people she passed in the street. She had received invitations from childhood friends but had turned them down. What could they possibly talk about? She didn't want to discuss her childhood, which included Léon, or her more recent past, which held Florian, Cosi, and Oriana.

But there was always la Rocque Varou.

He wasn't there. He has to come, Estelle told herself. He always does. She waited, leaning against the dolmen in the heat of the sun, the gorse around her smelling of milk and honey. Why did he not appear? Had she somehow conjured him out of the air, to do her bidding?

After an hour she dared stay no longer. Before she left, she walked around the menhir and looked at the sea below. It lay tranquil today, one smooth line where the water met the coast, limpid and bright. She imagined diving off the cliff, her body moving through the clear, warm air, plunging into the sparkling coolness below that curved around her, embracing and welcoming her. An errant gust of wind gave her a little push, and she involuntarily pressed herself back from the cliff edge against the dolmen's face.

Estelle smiled at the irony of her instinctive reaction. It

appeared she preferred to be buried alive. Touching the granite once more, she turned back to the town and Le Refuge. As she went, she picked wild flowers to take back with her: wild orchids, vetch, and tiny ferns. Maybe she could turn away Florian's anger at her absence if she came bearing gifts.

As she came in the garden gate, Florian was waiting for her in the old cane chair beneath the apple tree. His face came as a shock when she saw him: it was again the tight-skinned death-mask she had seen in Paris. Lately she had only been looking in apprehension for the hostility and suspicion she feared, which she now saw was there as well.

She thrust her bouquet before her, a peace-offering for a jealous lover. "For you, Florian, island flowers."

The face before her contorted into an expression of utter horror. Florian put his hands in front of his face and started to scream.

"Take them away! Are you trying to kill me? Is your lover trying to murder me? Deadly — They are trying to poison me!"

Frightened, baffled, Estelle could only think of saying, "They're not poisonous plants, Florian. Look, they're flowers!"

Cowering in the chair, his body shaking, he continued to scream in a macabre, whining wail that pierced the quiet air. "Snakes, vipers, scorpions! Take them away from me!"

Horror filled Estelle as she realized he was again hallucinating. She turned back and threw the flowers outside the gate, beyond the garden walls, then ran back to his side. Crouched at his feet, she tried to hold his hands, get him to look at her.

"Florian, look, they are gone. Do you really think I would harm you, when I care for you so much?"

Relieved, she saw Celestine come running out of the house. Florian was better with her when he was like this, and Estelle's presence only seemed to make matters worse. She moved back as the old woman bent over him, rocking him in her arms.

"Go, Estelle, leave him to me. There's nothing you can do for him, *petite fille*."

Nothing she could do for him. As she walked away from

them toward the house, Estelle was struck by the irony of Celestine's words. She who had set out to be his savior now seemed to be his persecutor.

At the same time, another thought occurred to her. Could it be that Florian was getting alcohol from somewhere? He was certainly behaving as if he were drinking again. Would the hallucinations be returning unless he were drinking? He asked for liquor all the time, but surely Celestine wouldn't be so foolish as to give him any. Angrily, Estelle shook her head. Impossible. The doctor himself had told Celestine that Florian must never drink again.

Wearily she climbed the stairs to her bedroom. Her closest companion seemed further than ever from being a true partner again to her, and the genius of la Rocque Varou had deserted her. She felt loneliness settling over her like a shroud. She crossed to the window as she always did and looked toward the harbor.

The *Nerine* was back. The cutter had been gone for a while, and its renewed presence restored a feeling of hope to her. Throwing herself onto the cushions of the window seat, she fixed her gaze upon it and thought of Léon. As Estelle did so, she realized what other thought was in her mind. She was imagining Florian fading away, weakening, disappearing from her life. Dead. Yes, for the first time, she wished he were dead.

Appalled, she watched fascinated as the idea rolled around in some long, dark corridor in her mind. She would never have contemplated killing him with her own hands, but she knew she would no longer struggle to help him survive. Softly, under her breath, she started to sing:

"Mauvaise jalousie que tu me fais du tor,
Me privait de la vie, faut que je souffre la mort,
Je l'ai bien merité il est indisputable,
Car ma cruauté jetois plus qu'execrable."

"Evil jealousy, how you have harmed me. . . . I must die because of my appalling cruelty."

So be it, if that is the only way of escape, thought Estelle. She turned back into the room and away from the *Nerine*.

Estelle heard Florian screaming again during the night and made her way swiftly along the dark corridors to his room. Celestine was already there, holding his hands and doing her best to reassure him. But Florian was pulling away from her, trying to tear at his face and hair.

For one moment, Estelle felt her own sanity shake as Cosimo's faceless face hovered in her mind, gaping and bloodied. This time there was fear in Celestine's expression as she watched Estelle sway and hold the doorpost.

"Go, Estelle, go back to bed."

Breaking again from Celestine's grasp, Florian now stretched out his hands toward Estelle. "Don't leave me. Star-lady, stay with me."

"It's all right, Celestine. You can leave him with me." Holding him against her, feeling the pathetic frailty of his body, the shudders that threatened to tear him apart, she felt only pity and love.

The hand that had pulled a coverlet over her seducer so long ago now stroked the forehead of her jailer. It wasn't as easy to free herself as Estelle had thought. It seemed as if she would be captive forever.

When dawn broke, Celestine found her sitting in the chair by the bed, staring into space. There was a set to her jaw and shoulders, and her hands were clasped firmly in her lap.

"*Ma p'tite,* you haven't slept all night!"

"No, I'll sleep now. I will be going out this afternoon."

Celestine looked at her warningly. "Should it — would it not be better if —"

"No, it would not."

Without another word, Estelle walked past the old woman and toward her own room. Lying on her bed, staring at the ceiling, she heard ringing in her ears over and over again what Florian had called out in the night from the secret depths of his dreaming.

"Cosi — Cosi — Cosi!"

Chapter Twenty-seven

THE RAIN STARTED as Estelle returned from her second fruitless trip. She had watched it coming across from the direction of Herm in a long black bank of clouds, the water beneath changing color as it passed. She waited until the rain reached the cliff face, soaking her face and hair in a matter of seconds. Her cloak billowing around her, the wind at her back, she made her way back to Le Refuge.

The walled garden was deserted, the wicker chair empty beneath the apple tree, forgotten in the rain. As she moved from the comparative shelter of the fruit trees near the gate, she saw old Luc scurrying as fast as his rheumatic legs would carry him from the main house to the garden door of the dower wing. There was something furtive about his scuttling progress that didn't seem entirely to do with the inclement weather.

She had been so blind! Breaking into a run, Estelle reached him as he made to close the long windows behind him. "*Attends,* Luc! Show me what you have there."

Grabbing his arm which he held under his coat, Estelle

pulled it out. Luc gasped in pain and fright, *"Nennin, princesse!"* A bottle dropped to the floor between them and broke.

Cognac from oncle Matthieu's cellar. The scent of the brandy rose and mingled with the smell of the summer rain on the garden outside. Fragrant as perfume, precious as gold.

"My God, Luc, it was you! Do you know what you have done? You have condemned him to death. You are killing him!"

"Never, not me! It is you who destroy him by keeping it from him, for I've seen him shake until he gets it. Then all is well — he recovers. It is you who destroy him, *princesse*!"

"You foolish old man," she said despairingly. "It may be too late now to save him because of you. He was getting better. Dear God, what have you done?"

There was a sound behind her. Florian stood in the doorway, his eyes fixed on the shattered bottle. "What have you done?" he repeated, unconsciously echoing her words. "You broke it. . . . Ah, no, you broke it!"

He lurched forward, throwing himself onto the floor between them, scrabbling among the glass shards with his bare hands. Blood sprang from his fingers and he cried out, putting them in his mouth and sucking the blood and brandy from them.

"Help me get him away before he hurts himself seriously." Estelle bent down but Florian pushed her back with a force that threw her against a table. As she fell, she saw old Luc standing there, transfixed. Florian started screaming.

"Do you know where she goes, Luc? She goes to meet her lover. Come foul or fair weather she goes! Did you know that, Luc? I was her lover once — Her husband gave her to me! Oh yes, and now she goes to meet her new man, de Polnay. Up on the cliffs, lying in the grass like a drab!"

Tears ran down Luc's face. He stood shaking his head, stretching out trembling hands to Florian, who still knelt before him on the floor. "*Nennin, m'sieu,* you do her wrong. She meets no one, certainly not de Polnay. He has someone else."

He put out his hand again, and this time Florian took it, the two of them staggering as he got to his feet. He allowed Estelle to come over to him, hold him on the other side, get him to a chair.

"Fetch a broom, Luc, and get Celestine to bring bandages."

As Luc swept and wept, Celestine clucked and cleaned Florian's bloodied hands. Estelle put the table she had knocked over to rights.

"I am wet," she said to Celestine. "I must go and change into dry clothes. Call me if you need me."

So there was "someone else," as Luc had said. Well, what should she have expected? Celibacy while onshore was not Leon's inclination, and Estelle had given him nothing to hope for from her.

When Florian screamed that night, Estelle didn't go to him. She heard Celestine running along the passage, calling out as she went.

Let Celestine be the one to hear him call out Cosi's name in the night. It wouldn't bring to her a phantasm with a hairless white body and raw flesh where his face should have been.

It could not have been many hours later that Estelle felt someone shaking her and calling her name. She found herself staring up at Celestine.

"Come quickly, Estelle. He is gone!"

"Dead? He is dead?" Estelle repeated, misunderstanding the old woman's cry.

"*Nennin,* he disappeared while I slept in the chair beside him. His bed is empty, his clothing gone!"

Estelle started to struggle out of bed, pull on some clothes. "Maybe he's wandering in the house somewhere. I'll help you look for him."

"I looked in the house before I woke you, *petite fille,* and Luc has searched the garden. He's nowhere to be found. Could he have gone into town, do you think?"

In that moment, Estelle knew with complete certainty where Florian had gone.

"I know where he will be. Luc can light me a lantern. You must go and tell oncle Matthieu, ask him to follow me. I may need his help this time — to avoid scandal, tell him." She was off, running down the stairs, calling out Luc's name.

Celestine's voice drifted after her. "But where shall I tell him you have gone?"

"To la Rocque Varou, Celestine."

Estelle met Luc coming in through the French windows, a hurricane lantern in his hand. He opened his mouth to speak, but she cut across the words, her eyes blazing in the light from the lamp, burning into the old man's face. "Did you tell him about la Rocque Varou?"

"Ouai, mais —"

Without explanation, she snatched the lamp from him, breaking off his protests and making for the gate in the garden wall.

There was still rain on the wind, but it wasn't the steady onslaught it had been earlier in the night. Clouds scudded across the moon's face and Estelle couldn't see any stars. "One of those nights we smugglers call 'the darks'." Would Léon be out there tonight, plying his secret trade? No, she thought, more likely safe in bed with his someone else. This time, she must manage on her own. The lantern held high, she pressed on as the lane turned into the exposed path that led to the cliffs, and the wind hit her with full force.

The lantern flickered ominously in the blast and threatened to go out. Estelle tried to shield it with her body from the main force of the gale. She had to have a light out here. There was no illumination from the stars, only intermittent moonlight, and no reassuring light from the window of a house. As she reached the cliff-top she started to call Florian's name, shaken suddenly in her certainty that he would have come here.

"Florian, where are you? It's Estelle. Darling Florian, answer me, please!"

She heard the crash and roar of the sea against the rocks below. A cloud raced across the face of the moon, and as it moved away she saw a figure crouching against the great menhir.

"Come to meet your lover, have you, star-lady?" Florian's voice was carried to her by the gale. "He hasn't come yet, but I'll wait for him. Then I'll take him over there, with me!"

Estelle brought down the lantern so she could see Florian's face. He was laughing. The thin lips moved back over his teeth, and the illusion of a death's head was complete.

"Florian, my love, you will wait in vain, you will wait forever! There is no one, there never has been anyone besides you. Only you, and no one else!"

He stood up suddenly, his thin shirt blown against his gaunt ribcage, his arms extended against the great rock. "Swear it then! Swear it on the life of de Polnay, out on a sea like this one! Take an oath on that body you say you haven't known!"

Estelle risked coming closer to him, holding up the lantern to illuminate her face. "Look at me, Florian. I swear on de Polnay's life that he is not nor ever has been my lover. There has been no one but you. No other man has ever made love to me, and with you alone I shared a marriage bed."

There was genuine joy now in the terrible smile, a release of tension in the gaunt frame.

"Cosi was no use to you."

"None."

"Nor to me once I had met you. I'm glad he died as he did. I still dream of killing him myself."

So that was the cry — the cry of a murderer, not a lover. Tears came to Estelle's eyes. "Oh, Florian, my love! How we have made each other suffer."

He didn't seem to hear her but to be pursuing some other thought. "I'm no use to you now, I keep you prisoner."

Estelle found herself passionately denying the thought that had been hers. "Never! I am where I want to be."

"No!" Florian started to move around the side of the menhir, his hands fumbling across the granite surface, his legs unsteady.

"Don't move, Florian. Come to me, come home with me." Breathless with fear, Estelle started toward him.

Florian broke into a tottering run that took him away from the comparative safety of the rock and into the full force of the gale. Estelle saw him stagger closer to the edge of the cliff.

Terrified that her pursuit would push him further, she stood still and put out her hand.

"Florian, think of the future, not of the past! Think of us together, forever!"

He was shaking his head slowly, smiling again at her the lazy, sensuous smile of the man who had taken her by force and stayed with her out of love.

"No use, Estelle. If I cannot have you again — and I cannot, I know that — I'll open the cage for both of us. It's my gift to you — I'll set you free!"

He threw wide his arms and looked up at the sky, shouting with laughter like a small boy suddenly enchanted by something wonderful.

"See the moon, Estelle! It shines for you, no one else. It shines for you, star-lady. It smiles on you!"

Startled, she looked at the moon as he waved his arms wildly, as if he were expecting to see . . . she knew not what.

In that moment, Florian was gone. No sound, no scream, no cry. Just the noise of the waves, a gull's cry, and the cliff empty where he had stood.

When oncle Matthieu and Celestine found Estelle, she was lying flat on the ground, her hands clinging to the grass tufts bordering the cliff's edge. The lantern had gone out, and the first gray streaks of dawn showed through the black storm-clouds.

As they approached, Estelle turned her head and smiled at them, gravely, lovingly. "I have prayed for him. He is at peace now." Then calmly she stood up, brushing her skirt and cloak with infinite care.

"Let us go back. There is nothing more to be done here."

Speechless, Celestine and Matthieu watched her move ahead of them, walking slowly but steadily along the cliff path back to Le Refuge. After a moment's hesitation they turned and followed her.

Chapter Twenty-eight

FLORIAN'S BODY WASHED UP on the shores of Fermain Bay a few weeks later. The constable in charge of the case was gentle with Estelle, having been apprised of the danger to her fragile state of mind. Two faceless horrors had been adjudged too much for her to handle, so it was oncle Matthieu who had formally identified the body. He returned blanched and shaken.

Estelle wrote to Uncle William and Aunt Dorothea, explaining the circumstances of Florian's death. She didn't know if they were aware of where Florian had been, and she herself hadn't been in touch with them since the Orsini affair.

A few weeks later there was a reply from Uncle William's lawyer. Estelle was astonished to discover that Florian had made a will leaving her the sole beneficiary of such estate as he had. Oncle Matthieu took it upon himself to deal with the legal details, grimly determined to recoup as much as possible to add to Estelle's depleted fortune. He had already discovered that Cosimo had left her nothing, for there had been nothing to leave; his pride in his business acumen had been severely shaken.

Estelle knew that Florian's estate would not amount to much. There was a high price attached to such a lifestyle as theirs had been. The costly gifts to Uncle William and Aunt Dorothea had been investments to insure Florian would be their sole heir.

She was not surprised to learn that Uncle William wished to have no further communication with her. "She has betrayed her country" was apparently how he had expressed it to his solicitor.

Estelle had thought that the aftermath of Florian's suicide would be a feeling of withdrawal from the world, the flesh, and the devil. Instead, she was filled with a desperate longing to break out of her isolation, to prove to herself that she was alive, still young and beautiful.

One balmy summer afternoon, she sat down at the rosewood escritoire in the salon and wrote to Léon de Polnay.

Cher Léon,
You have heard, I imagine, of Florian's death. The verdict was suicide while of unsound mind, but he did it in a moment of sanity, to set me free. I know because I was there, and that is what he told me. He also freed himself from a terrible malady he could never have conquered. The seeds of its destruction were there when I first knew him. For Florian, there was only boredom or intoxication, and nothing in between.

I am free, but there is such a difference between freedom and free time. I know now that I am not a seeker of extremes. I want the middle ground, where a flame can burn steadily without consuming everything in its path.

I have not really said what I want to say, and I suppose I am hoping you will read between the lines. I have to tell you, Léon, that what you intended came to pass. Regretting what might have been, I now have reason to hope there are better things to come.

Estelle Gastineau

Léon came through the gate into the walled garden, as he had done so often all those years ago. He stood there for a moment and looked across the lawn toward the house with its fine Georgian facade, so different from the accumulation of architectural styles that generations of de Polnays had given to their home. But both were built on cellars of brandy and rum, port and fine wines, ships that sailed like the wind, and men who had been the *beau idéal* of generations of law-abiding citizens.

Through the long windows of the salon he saw a movement, a wisp of pale blue silk, a hand white against dark mahogany. Estelle. He hadn't replied to her letter, hadn't known if he would come until he found his feet walking up Hauteville. Or so he had told himself.

The scent of the small white rambling roses drifted toward him on the soft breeze. *Jeune fille en fleur*. Estelle, my darling, he mused. What a terrible thing innocence can be. Léon picked one of the blooms that was just breaking into flower and strode into the salon before he could change his mind.

Against that dark interior she glowed, blond hair like a nimbus, the pale blue of the dress deepening the already dark blue eyes, now widened in shock, staring at the tiger-eyes of the man who stood there, a white rose held out in his hand.

A shadow of some emotion he couldn't interpret moved across her face. Putting out her hand as if to stop him, Estelle said, "You startled me."

"I'm sorry, but I come in answer to a letter."

The hand now welcomed him, and her smile was glorious, full of promise and happiness. "I'm glad. Is that for me?"

"Who else, madame?"

The silk rustled softly around Estelle as she approached and took the rose from him, holding it to her face. "Beautiful. I'll tuck it in my belt until I can give it a vase of its own."

"Allow me." Léon took it from her and bent forward, tucking it into the ruched waistband, feeling the tiny thorns prick against his fingers. When he looked up again, her face was close to him. I have no words, he thought. What can I tell her? Gently he placed his hand against the silken fold of hair at her neck and kissed her, terrified she would turn away from him.

There was a stillness about her for a moment. Then it was gone, her slender form swaying against him, her arms around his waist caressing him. It would be better, Léon knew, if Estelle rejected him, for he assuredly could not resist her. He had meant first to tell her of the trap that had closed around him. Now it seemed impossible. He had spent his young manhood giving in to every temptation, and it was unthinkable to change character at this moment, when he wanted her so much.

He kissed the corner of her jaw, the angle of her neck, and heard her whisper his name. As she moved her lips to his, he felt his body shake at the passion he sensed flowing from her, released by his kisses.

"Estelle . . . there's something I have to tell you. We must talk, *petite étoile.*"

There, he had managed to say it, but instantly he regretted his decision. Estelle turned away from him, and he saw the fear of rejection in her eyes. Before he could speak or reach out to her, she cried out, "It was so hard to write, so hard to ask you — to tell you — and what will you now tell me? That you didn't mean what I felt between us in the cave, in the darkness, when you said it could never be! Léon, it can. That's what I want to tell you — it can. But I see now your feelings have changed. Forgive me. Why should I think it would be otherwise? Why should I expect you to be faithful to an impossible dream!"

Anguish filled him. She was right. He hadn't been faithful to an impossible dream, and he regretted it more bitterly than ever when he saw her before him. All he could do now was fight for it, fight to free himself.

"I love you, Estelle!" The words were torn from him, words he had never said to any woman.

She believed him — thank God, she believed him. Léon saw it in her eyes and then heard it in her voice when she replied, "Then no words, enough of accusations, lies. Hold me, that's all I want."

He was lost. She put her arms around him, her lips against his face. He felt the resolution go from him again and tried to put his guilt into words before his will failed him completely. "No, my love, I want more — oh, not just what you think — but it means I must put my life to rights before I can make any promises. I wanted to kiss you, I'll not deny that. But we must stop now, or I shall forget why I came."

Beneath his hands the fair hair had fallen loose and hung behind her, soft as the silk she wore.

"This is why you came," she whispered. "I must know that I can give myself to you and that you will love me tomorrow . . . and the day after that. I must know that it is me, Estelle, that you care for. That your feelings are not altered if I am innocent, guilty, a virgin, or a whore."

The final word, so unexpected from her lips, filled Léon with pain. "I don't understand you. How could I ever think about you like that? How can I promise you such a thing?"

In answer, Estelle took his hand and led him through the deserted house. As they climbed the stairs, he was filled with longing and despair. He would tell her. . . . Of course he would, but he would let his resolve be strengthened by making love to her first.

Léon closed the door of her room behind them and picked her up in his arms, carrying her the few steps to the bed. As he removed the silk dress, Estelle's eyes stayed on his face with an easy naturalness that roused him beyond any show of maidenly reluctance or sexual excess. She was behaving as if this was how things should have been between them, the way it had been intended all along. She extended her hand and started to remove his jacket, her voice caressing his name as her hand stroked him, moving across his body and around his waist.

"Léon, this was what I wanted all those years ago, when the touch of you frightened me and made me feel I wanted to forget all I had been taught was good and right and proper —"

Words failed her. She gasped as Léon's lips brushed her breasts, his hands ran the length of her spine, pulling her against him. When he spoke, the surprise in his voice sounded almost like anger.

"You wanted this! Ah, Estelle, I who thought myself such an

expert on women read your fear as rejection. I thought you were cold."

"Cold?" She, too, now sounded angry at the misunderstanding and ignorance that had torn them apart. Suddenly she pushed him away from her, her hand hard against his body. "Don't you see? I was desperate for you. Oh, Léon, you were as ignorant as I was, as guilty as I was! No, not guilty, neither of us guilty but innocents, babes in arms. I now know that a cold woman can give herself easily, for it means nothing to her. *Dieu,* Léon, if you have no heart it's easy to give it away! It's a trick, an illusion. If you know you have a heart to give — just one, just once — it's a fearful thing, not to be taken lightly. I may be innocent no longer, but my heart is for you as it has always been."

He also knew only too well how easy it was for the heartless to give themselves, for indeed they gave nothing. They took and perverted and sucked one dry. It had taken corruption to show him what true love was. Or maybe it was the beautiful woman in his arms who said she loved him. If he had had resolutions, he could not remember them, not with Estelle's hands stroking his hips, his thighs, as she pushed the rest of his clothing from him.

"*Dieu,* I was blind! How could I have seen you as cold?"

To Léon's amazement he now heard laughter in her voice, even as he moved against her, penetrated her. She was laughing, crying, pulling him closer to her as if he could not be too deeply within her.

"Léon de Polnay, you are a man of light loves, frivolous liaisons! You know nothing of a woman like me. Do you know why? Because you have been frightened of such passion as you and I have between us. If I was cold, then so were you!"

"Cold!" The word roared from him and then he stopped her laughing, crying mouth with his own. Léon felt her body arch beneath him, forgot everything else: words, explanations, the profound complication from which he had struggled unsuccessfully to extricate himself as the climax hit them both.

In each other's arms now, cradled, safe. Léon touched her

cheek gently, felt the curve of cheekbone beneath the delicate skin. *"Jeune fille en fleur."*

"Still?" She held a strand of his dark hair and felt the strength and vitality of him in its texture against her fingertips.

"Always for me. No, *jeune femme en fleur.* Not a girl, but a woman, Estelle. You explode like a shooting star."

"Remember, I want the middle ground. I don't want to be consumed."

"You won't be, for we'll both feed on this fire forever." He sat up on the bed and glanced out of the window.

"I can see the *Nerine* from here, Léon. I used to watch your comings and goings, see the light off Jethou."

"Did you? Ah yes, there she is — my other beautiful woman." His other beautiful woman. He turned toward her, her face clouded. "Estelle, *cherie,* you said not to talk, but there is something I have to do before I can make any promises to you."

"I know." She was smiling, calmly stroking his arm.

"And yet you still —"

"Yes. Now you and I have made love, it will be easier for you."

He was certain now she hadn't guessed the truth. She must think it was one of those light loves, those frivolous liaisons she had so rightly accused him of. After what had now passed between them, after the magic of their lovemaking, he knew he could not tell her the truth. He could only pray she was right and that some of her magic — and his resolution — stayed with him. How he wished he could take her with him, her blond beauty a magic charm against the dark pit into which he feared he might fall again! He was so weak, so easily corrupted by the sins of the flesh.

"Go and set yourself free." It sounded so easy. He said no more but turned back to her, pressing her close, imprinting into her body's memory the feel of the breasts, her thighs, her buttocks against the palms of his hands, as he made love to her again.

Léon left before Luc and Celestine returned, anxious they

should not see him. Estelle thought it was out of consideration for her and was touched by his delicacy. He still could not tell her why. He was sure the servants would not have told her, for fear of disturbing again her peace of mind. They might feel differently, however, if they knew he had reappeared in Estelle's life.

As Léon de Polnay rode away through the gathering dusk, another feeling grew within him. The solemnity and passion of Estelle's commitment and his own response awakened within him an emotion he feared far more than the nature of the involvement that lay before him at le clos de Polnay. "Can I change?" he thought. "Will I not betray even such a woman as this?"

What he had also not foreseen was that Estelle would greet Celestine and Luc on their return with news of his visit, her voice ringing with happiness. She had thought they would be pleased that she was planning to make Léon de Polnay the one she had chosen.

Estelle was stunned by their reaction. Jaws agape, they stood frozen to the spot, staring at their radiant mistress.

"Léon de Polnay came here?"

"Yes, I just told you so. What's wrong?"

"But, Estelle, *petite fille,* he has — he is —" Celestine threw up her hands as if she despaired of putting into words what she had to say. Luc turned around and left the room, muttering under his breath.

"All's well, Celestine," said Estelle reassuringly. "I know he has things to sort out before he can make any promises to me. He has told me that."

Relief crossed the old woman's face. "*Dieu merci!* Did he tell you that —"

Swiftly, Estelle interrupted her. "No, it's best I don't know what these things are, for I have seen what jealousy can do. Let Léon put his house in order and come back to me."

Estelle crossed over to the windows of the salon and looked at the garden through which she had seen him come back to her, a white rose in his hands. Soon, he would come to her once more. This time he would be free, untrammelled, his "someone else" part of the past. She was his future, and he hers.

Behind her Celestine and Luc looked at each other. The old man opened his mouth as if he would say more, but Celestine placed a finger to her lips. Together they stood and looked at the slender figure outlined against the night-dark garden beyond the salon windows.

The days grew shorter as the late summer sun sank earlier behind the hills of Saint Peter Port. The corn was gathered in, and the month of September moved on to Michaelmas and the feast of Saint Michael the Archangel, the Christian successor to Neptune, beloved by all seafarers.

Léon de Polnay had not returned to Le Refuge. Estelle had neither written nor tried to see him, for she knew it had to be his decision. She had committed herself; now he must do the same without coercion. Eventually, however, she brought herself to speak to Celestine.

"Celestine, it is evident you know something of Léon's circumstances. I now feel I should know more of what it is he has to do."

Celestine, however, had had a few weeks for reflection and had changed her tune. She refused adamantly to enlighten Estelle. "I now think it best you know nothing, Estelle. It will take time, that much I know. *Ouai, ma fille,* you'll have to give him time."

Time, thought Estelle. Give him my understanding, give him my love, give him my body, give him time. Time was what she couldn't give him, for it was running out. Or at least it was moving fast toward something she couldn't control, something she wanted and yet feared. . . .

Once, just once. All the horror stories Celestine had told, all the dreadful warnings she gave me, all come true. In spite of herself, she smiled and hugged her arms tight around her body. *"En basse fosse,"* she whispered to herself, *"en basse fosse."*

Resolution came to her out of nowhere, a change of heart. Léon had a right to know, after all. "I *will* go. I want to see his face when I tell him I am carrying his child."

Maturin l'Eustace and Marie's brother, Michel Priaulx, made frequent trips to the clos de Polnay. She would get one of them to take her tomorrow, while her resolve was still strong, but she would say nothing to Luc or Celestine. She didn't want to risk the possibility of oncle Matthieu being involved in any way.

Early the next day she left Le Refuge and found Marie's brother at Les Halles, preparing for the day's work. When she offered him a fee for the trip, he was easily persuaded to leave his stall in charge of his eldest son. They departed in a high good humor, which suited Estelle's mood of hope and optimism.

The cart rattled through the autumn countryside of brown and gold, the scent from the cider presses filling the air as they passed the farms. The first batch of cider would now be ready, *le meis d'octobre.* With it came the first of the winter *veilles,* those friendly get-togethers when the country people met together before the fire, when the day's work was done, beneath the light of the crasset lamp.

Michel talked with happy anticipation of the *veille* he was to attend that night: of laughter and gossip, tea and cider, rhubarb pie and apple cake. At his words, Estelle felt the contentment grow within her, love for this secure island, this middle ground which she had now found. Her child would be born into this safe circle of life, with roots deep in the fertile soil of stability. Her joys would be those of her ancestors, joys she thought she had lost forever.

At the top of the hill that looked over the clos de Polnay, she felt a sense of homecoming. A wisp of smoke curled up from one of the chimneys, and she could smell its pungent fragrance drifting toward them.

"I'll leave you at the front of the house, madame, and take the cart round the back to the kitchen."

"Thank you, Monsieur Priaulx. I'm very grateful to you."

Ranulph remembered her. The great dog leaped at her, whining with pleasure, trying to lick her face as she laughed and fended him off. "Careful, *petit chien,* be careful with me now, with those great paws of yours. Where is your master?"

Ranulph's ears pricked as if trying to understand her. The dog looked at Estelle and then at the door beneath the double arch.

"You think he's in there? Let's see if you're right."

The door wasn't locked. Estelle swung it open easily and stood in the doorway. The room seemed dim after the golden autumn sunlight; and the air was musty and oppressive. Beside her, at the full length of his chain, Ranulph growled softly, teeth bared.

"*Qu'est que t'as, petit chien?*" As she bent to stroke his head Estelle heard a sound from the far side of the room. Someone was laughing, a low steady sound with a metallic note. It was the timbre of a voice she remembered, cracked and flawed like the woman who owned it.

Oriana.

Chapter Twenty-nine

ORIANA WAS ON THE *LIT DE FOUAILLE*, close to the great chimney, lounging back on her elbow. She wore damson satin and rubies. Her black hair was threaded with ribbons of scarlet and gold, twisted around her head in elaborate coils. Stretched out in front of her, her feet were bare, startlingly white like the skin of her face and half-exposed breasts. It was like seeing her again through the moving fireplace at Aberville House.

The laughter ceased. In the broken, throaty voice Estelle remembered so well, she said, "I saw you coming. I knew you would come, Estelle."

Silence fell between them, heavy and ugly as lead. Beside Estelle, Ranulph continued to growl deep in his throat. Oriana spoke again. "Are you not going to ask me how I came to be here?"

"You are doubtless going to tell me."

Estelle was surprised at the sound of her own voice. It sounded clear and cool, unmoved at the devastation she felt inside.

"Of course. I became ill in prison and they released me on

condition I never return again to France. We'll see about that. I have friends at court, as the saying goes. Besides, the governor at Saint Lazare will be so desolated if I don't return. He did so enjoy having me at his mercy — playing the helpless slave is so entertaining! Things proved to be . . . difficult in England, so I decided to visit you. And I'm afraid I was unexpectedly detained by your gentleman smuggler. It was all so simple, really."

No. It had not been simple, but Oriana would never reveal to this hated rival who stood before her the extent of her suffering. Estelle must continue to see her as the *femme maîtresse*, the manipulator who held all the cards, won every game she played.

Oriana had indeed been ill, but as a result of the excesses that she had hoped would give her either freedom or preferential treatment. After one beating too many, she had been taken to hospital. Horrified officials arranged her release in an attempt to hush up the affair.

While recovering in hospital, she had learned of Florian's escape and had summoned Albert Jolivet to her bedside. What he told her filled her with a bitter hatred toward both Florian and Estelle that sped her recovery quite as effectively as medicaments or loving care. Fuelled by this emotion, she made her way to England and to Bostock Hall. Out of genuine antipathy or prudent discretion she had found that all other doors were closed to her.

The interview with Uncle William and Aunt Dorothea had been predictably unpleasant and negative but informative. Florian, she discovered, was in Guernsey.

"How," she asked in genuine bewilderment, "did that sheltered little island girl arrange all this?"

Trembling with outrage, Uncle William had replied, "By usin' some island reprobate — friend of the family's. Damned Frenchie and smuggler to boot, so I gather. They came here from London to question me — *me!* — about 'im. I knew less than they did."

"They" were the authorities investigating the original assassination attempt. They had not pursued their inquiries when they found that Léon de Polnay was not connected with the conspiracy and that the French were not anxious to have Florian d'Aberville returned to their shores.

Oriana returned to London to face ostracism and financial chaos. Driven by vengeance and financial necessity, she made her way to Southampton and was on the steamer for Guernsey in a matter of days.

Within the first twenty-four hours of Oriana's arrival, a chambermaid at the inn where she was staying had told her of Estelle's earlier engagement to Léon de Polnay and had waxed rhapsodic over his beauty.

From that moment Oriana's course of action was decided. Piquancy was added by the girl's final remark.

"They say they still love each other, but Estelle will never leave the Englishman's side — not while he's so ill, poor man. Poor Estelle! It's all so *sad*, madame."

Then and only then had it been simple. Everything had fallen into her lap so beautifully. Oriana had arrived late at le clos de Polnay, ostensibly to make inquiries before she intruded on Estelle's suffering. Léon de Polnay, being a gentleman, had not turned her away into the night. Besides, the gentleman was slightly drunk and jealous beyond anything he had thought possible, raging inside at his inability to conquer his pain.

Weeping affectingly over her wine and disarmingly agreeing with much of what Estelle had told Léon about her, she nevertheless gave a carefully tailored version of Florian and Estelle's affair. Her host was only too anxious to believe her.

As he passed the guest-room that night, Léon could hear her sobbing. When he opened the door and saw the white skin, the black hair against the pillow, the eyes burning into him with what he took to be grief, he had not hesitated to step forward and comfort her. Within a matter of minutes he was assuaging their joint distress in the way that had come easiest to him all his adult life. Locked in each other's arms they had expiated their rage and jealousy in an explosion of lust which both had found amazingly consoling.

Once tasted, Léon de Polnay found himself addicted. Besides, Oriana seemed so uncomplicated after Estelle. Her attitude to their relationship appeared very much like the one Léon had thought of as his own, in the past. "I can give you experiences you have never had, Léon. Then you can go back to whichever milquetoast island girl you choose." It seemed the perfect solution to his dislike of emotional involvement, the perfect salve for his wounded pride.

It was not long after Oriana had arrived that the news reached le clos de Polnay that Florian had committed suicide.

Léon would never forget the moment he told her. It was as if the smooth white skin of her face had cracked open before his eyes like an eggshell, and he saw for the first time what lay beneath.

Pacing the floor in front of the great hearth, whose warmth she craved even in midsummer, arms tightly clasped around her body, Oriana crooned over and over again, "Now I have her, now I have her, now I have her."

Too late, Léon realized his place in the scheme of things. "All for revenge?" he asked.

"Of course," she had replied. "Why? Did you think I loved you?" And she had laughed in his face. Revulsion hit him, as quick and hot as the desire he had felt the first night he had touched her.

"Get out," he had ordered her.

"Oh, I will . . . when *I* want to. Otherwise, I will have so much to tell, about cellars and secret beaches, and the smuggling of felons out of France. Oh — and the direct involvement of Estelle da Gamba."

Estelle's letter had arrived not long afterward, and Léon had been unable to resist the invitation it had conveyed. He had wondered if he would discover that his feeling for her had gone when he saw her again. It had always been like that for him in the past, and it would have been convenient if history had repeated itself.

He discovered instead the inconvenient truth: that for once he had found a woman he could not simply take and leave. For a man of his temperament, this was as frightening a discovery as the revelation of Oriana's true nature had been. When he had returned to le clos de Polnay, he had renewed his liaison with Oriana. He had not forgotten his revulsion; he had taken refuge in it.

Now, standing in the doorway and watching the two women face each other across the room, death seemed like a release to him. Anything rather than this.

"What are you doing here, Estelle?"

At Léon's voice Estelle swung around, eyes wide, her composure close to cracking for the first time. She buried her fingers deep in the fur on Ranulph's neck and answered him, carefully controlling her voice.

"I came to see you. I didn't know your someone else would be under your roof. I didn't know she would be one of those persons *de tchi qu'nou n' dit rian.*"

There was a laugh from the *lit de fouaille*. "How quaint! Just what your men call me, de Polnay. What primitive peasants your island friends are!"

Leon swung round on the dark figure crouching on the rough couch, anger in his voice. "*Tais-toi!* When you say that, you insult me, too."

The selfishness of his response gave Estelle the resolve she needed. "Oriana is right, Léon. We are primitive, we Guernsey peasants. She might do well to remember that. If you arouse the fear of a primitive people, the outcome can be savage and terrible."

"Are you threatening me, Estelle?" Oriana's voice seemed to purr with pleasure.

"Estelle —"

Before Léon could continue, she checked him, holding up her hand. "No. Fetch Michel de Priaulx and tell him I must leave immediately. I will wait for him outside."

He saw it was useless to argue. Besides, what did he have to argue about? He couldn't even promise to throw this black witch out of his house. God knew the men had cajoled him, cursed him, threatened him over her presence, and he had done nothing. He turned on his heel and left the room.

As Estelle moved toward the open front door, the voice stopped her. It hissed now, carrying across the intervening space like the whine of the wind when it builds at the height of a storm.

"You ruined everything, Estelle, and now I'll ruin everything for you. You and de Polnay are finished, and I, too, will spit him out. There are other amusements available to me here — but you'll not have him."

Estelle looked at Oriana, at the smooth white face that had fed on serpents' eggs and hypocrisy and lies. She forced herself to speak. "We have a saying, Oriana, we primitive peasants. *L'amour hâle pûs que chent boeufs.* Can you encompass the meaning in your Parisian French? Love pulls more than one hundred oxen. I believe that. It conquers because it's stronger than hatred. You cannot win."

The eyes of the other woman were like slits. "Are you challenging me, Estelle?"

"Yes. I suppose I am."

Oriana threw back her head in soundless laughter, a bejewelled hand clutching her throat. "My dear Estelle, are you still so hopelessly naive? Or is this just a performance, a charming act you are putting on for my benefit?"

"Come, Ranulph." Estelle pulled on the dog's chain, and he came with her through the arched doorway into the warm autumn light outside.

Michel Priaulx's cart was already coming around the side of the house, and Estelle saw that Marie was with her brother. Her usually expressionless face was looking anxiously in Estelle's direction.

"You shouldn't have come here, madame, but Michel didn't know. I was just going to fetch you myself when the master came. This is a bad place now, and I'll leave if the other one doesn't go soon."

"When did she arrive, Marie?"

"Not long after the master got back from Saint-Malo with you. It's disgraceful, the goings-on! She should beware, that one. The men hate her."

"Léon's men?"

"*Ouai.* They should be off again on their business, but he goes nowhere. It's as if he's frightened to be with her and frightened to be without her."

Michel Priaulx shifted uneasily from one foot to the other. "Eh, Marie, you tell me to be gone, so let us go. It does no good to keep madame standing here." He put out his hand and helped Estelle into the cart.

It was Estelle who broke the silence between them, a few minutes into their journey. "Monsieur Priaulx, would you please stop when we get to Saint Martin's church?"

He looked surprised, but nodded in agreement. "If you wish, madame."

There she was, keeping her perennial vigil by the churchyard gate. Ageless, powerful, la Gran'mère du Chimquière. What should she offer her?

"Here, madame, give her this." Michel Priaulx had understood. He reached back into the cart under some sacks and brought out an apple, ripe and glowing, two crisp leaves still clinging to its stem.

Estelle pulled out a piece of blue ribbon threaded through a fichu she was wearing and tied it to the stem of the apple.

Michel Priaulx nodded approvingly. "Good. Go and lay it at her feet."

Estelle did as she was told. She knelt before the dolmen and placed the apple in one of the cup-like hollows at her feet. "Look after him, gran'mère. And I say a prayer to you for the child that you and I alone know I carry."

Was it her imagination, or did she genuinely feel the gust of warmth that seemed to emanate from the figure before her? Estelle put out her hand and gently touched the stone, feeling something like a current streaming through her fingers.

"So be it." She looked up into the strong face. Did that powerful, maternal gaze now seem malevolent through some trick of the light, she wondered? Why was it that it seemed to her to be directed against those who would harm her and not against herself?

"*Viens,* madame, the holy stone has heard you."

She didn't ask Michel Priaulx how he knew that. She only knew he was right.

V'la une fière perruque à débouquer! Here's a fine wig to untangle! There really wasn't much to be gained in expressing it more strongly than that, although Celestines' words seemed comically inadequate. After all, what words were there to encompass what had happened?

She had never thought of Oriana, and the islanders didn't know the significance of the black-haired woman at le clos de Polnay. All they knew was that Léon de Polnay seemed bewitched. What was the use of telling Celestine that?

"Forget him, *petite fille,* put him out of your life. He has given you grief and sorrow once before. You almost lost your mind with all that happened to you."

Estelle turned toward her old nurse, who was pouring some warm water for her into the basin on the washstand. I must tell Celestine, she thought. I can trust her to keep silent, and she will guess soon enough.

"He has given me more than grief and sorrow, *nou-nou.* He has given me his child."

There was a crash as the heavy pitcher came down hard on the marble-topped stand. Celestine's face was white, her hands shaking.

"Oh, no, Estelle! You cannot mean . . . Have you —"

Gently, Estelle took the old woman's hands in hers and led her to the bed, where she sat her down and put her arms around her. "Yes, I do mean it. I have and I'm sure. Now, you mustn't worry for me, because I'm happy about it. We must now do what's best for the child. But not a word to anyone, you understand?"

Celestine rocked back and forth, moaning to herself. "*Ma petite Estelle,* what will happen to you? What will become of us?"

"Nothing, Celestine, you'll see. No one will throw me in Castle Cornet, I promise you. You will be a nurse again and I a mother."

"But a child should have a father. Oh, what will he do without a father?"

"He or she has a father. It is Léon de Polnay. I know that my child will not have to do without a father."

"Oh, my child, how can you know that?"

Estelle took Celestine's face gently between her hands and turned her toward her. "Because la Gran'mère du Chimquière told me so. Now listen. I will have to see Doctor Corbet, but we'll make no more plans for the time being. This is between you and me. No one else knows."

"Not even Léon?"

"Certainly not even Léon."

When Celestine left her, Estelle left the lamp burning a while. It was easier to feel confident while the lamplight illuminated the bedroom, cradling the bed in a warm pool of golden light and creating the illusion of an autumnal sun. The moonlight brought only Florian's death-mask face, and the darkness only Oriana's wax-white beauty.

Chapter Thirty

"*LA BELLE VEUVE* WALKS THE CLIFFS every day, *dit-on.*"

"Maybe she goes to meet the ghost of the one who died there."

"Who knows? They say he was her lover."

"It's no dead lover she meets up there. It's a live one, him from Hauteville."

But she didn't. Not until after September, when he came back from France, from giving his aging mistress, Juliette Drouet, her poor little dose of annual happiness.

Back in his "palace" in Hauteville the poet felt again the vision and direction that the island had given to his literary genius in his middle and old age. He redeposited Juliette at her own charming house, La Fallu, and began once more his daily ritual of sea-bathing and walking on the cliffs in all weathers.

He felt pleasure when he saw Estelle walking past the menhir, stopping a moment, and then moving on. She looked across the open expanse of gorse and grass and smiled when she saw him.

"You are returned."

She was more beautiful than he remembered, even after refreshing his eyes with the beauty of the women of Europe. There was a ripeness and yet a remoteness about her that appealed to his love of contrast and the unexpected.

"Of course. I return, a voluntary exile, to this rock lost in the sea. Paradise lost, paradise regained. Can you walk for a while? It's too cold to stand still for long."

She bowed her head in agreement, and they walked silently for a while before she spoke. "Do you wish to know the outcome of my . . . expedition?"

"The whole island seems to know. Your feelings are yours to reveal if you wish, madame."

"My husband is dead. So is my lover. Now the corruption and degradation I shed with those deaths touches another. Strangest of all, I still want him despite it. He betrays me, and yet I understand. I want to free him."

"Perhaps he doesn't want to be freed. Have you thought of that?"

"Yes, but I still feel I am bound to try."

"I warn you that our destiny and our wishes are almost always at odds. Still, you have much on your side. You are beautiful — that unfair advantage the gods give to some women — and you have already passed through the fire. And he may yet learn by himself that the numbing of feeling into insensibility isn't the same as enjoyment."

"Or happiness . . . or fulfillment."

"Let's settle on the lesser word for the time being. How do you see yourself, madame? As his fate, his savior, his nemesis?"

"As the mother of his child. Let's settle on the lesser words for the time being."

She heard him rumble with laughter. "Hmm, beauty and wit. A formidable combination, especially with what you have just told me. Every man wants to feel he will be immortal."

"Do you?"

He stopped walking for a moment and turned and faced her, his great white beard blowing back against his face. "Madame,

I *am* immortal. I am both a god and a victim of the gods. I am Olympio."

"We are all victims of the gods."

"Aha, the trick is to be a god as well! Good and evil, corruption and innocence — opposites can both exist in the same being."

She pushed back the strands of hair from her face as they whipped in the wind, and he wondered if they had caused the tears he saw.

In a quiet voice she replied, "Lost innocence can never be regained, I know that."

"Then you must remember that, madame, if you have a daughter." There was grief in his face, as if at the memory of some personal loss.

Both were silent as they walked back along the cliff, for the wind in their faces would have snatched their voices away. Estelle needed no more words, for the poet had altered her vision, as he had done before. She knew now that she couldn't tell Léon about his child. He had to want her in the frailty of her mortality, not for the immortality she carried within her.

At Celestine's insistence Estelle returned no more to la Rocque Varou. There was gossip starting in the town about her meetings with "that one from Hauteville House," and people might possibly think she was carrying his child. The pregnancy would not be apparent for another month or so, and Estelle hoped to conceal it until the spring from prying eyes. It was not so much the scandal she feared, as the news getting back to Léon. She felt a primitive terror when she thought of Oriana finding out and prayed that would not happen before the child was born.

Toward the end of October, after a visit to Doctor Corbet, Estelle decided to walk back to Le Refuge rather than have the carriage meet her. At the foot of the High Street she caught a glimpse between two buildings of the boats bobbing on the calm waters of the harbor and found her feet turning down toward the Esplanade.

The *Nerine* was there, as she knew from her window, and had been for many a long week. If Léon didn't take the cutter to sea soon, he would undoubtedly be there until the spring, apart from making the occasional short trip to Saint-Malo. Remembering Marie's comments about his men, their discontent and fears, Estelle wondered at the winter of discontent there would be if the crew remained on shore to kick their heels in Saint Sampson, in Torteval, or in Castel.

As if in answer to her thoughts, she suddenly saw the head of Pierre Gosselin as he came back up the other side of the sea wall. Before Estelle could turn away up High Street, he saw her and called out.

"*Wharro,* madame! A moment of your time." He came running across the road, tripping clumsily over his heavy boots.

"Monsieur Gosselin?"

"A word with you, madame. It's urgent." Without waiting for a reply, he indicated a small bootmaker's shop up the road. "There — Colin Briard is a good friend of mine. If we went there, it would be out of the wind and out of earshot."

Inside the tiny store, he greeted the small, heavily bearded proprietor and introduced Estelle. The man looked at her with undisguised curiosity. "Ah, madame, I know your uncle well. Go through, Pierre, go through."

In the small back room, Pierre Gosselin indicated she should sit down and without further ado began to speak. "Madame, there's much trouble brewing." He paused, as if expecting her to respond. When she didn't, he plunged desperately on. "The woman destroys him, and she destroys us all. She takes our captain, our livelihood. And if that's not enough, she has started on the young ones." He stopped and nervously started to turn his woollen cap round and round in his hands.

"Forgive me, madame. This is not nice for a lady to hear, but things are bad. She has bewitched young Paul Le Marchant. I'm sure she has already had him, although he denies it."

Estelle looked at his sweating, plump face and reminded him, "You called me a witch once, Monsieur Gosselin. Do you expect one witch to fight another? Do you want me to use charms and incantations? Haven't you tried salt or quicksilver or heated iron filings over the fire?"

She could see he was now angry and so continued more gently, "Léon de Polnay has to exorcise himself, and he will do so. Or she will do it herself, for it sounds as if she is already bored with her game. She is easily bored and has to move on to other amusements. Even young Paul will be left alone eventually."

Pierre Gosselin swayed on the hard wooden chair in agitation and hit his knee with his cap. "That's not good enough for us, madame, waiting for that black witch to finish her game. It's not that easy to find work at this time of the year. I rage inside when I think of how we sat around all summer, waiting for Léon de Polnay to come to his senses."

Estelle stood up and started to move back toward the door into the shop. "There's nothing I can do, monsieur. I'm sorry, but there's nothing."

Pierre Gosselin's shout filled the tiny space. "*Dieu,* madame, you owe him that much! If he hadn't helped you, this would never have happened. Have you thought of that? And what purpose did that serve? Going to fetch a drunken lunatic who throws himself off la Rocque Varou at full moon! You joined a nest of vipers, Estelle Gastineau, and you brought them here!"

Wordlessly, she shook her head and turned from him. His raised voice followed her as she made her way past a gaping Colin Briard.

"We will do it. We'll do it ourselves! Be warned, madame, her time has run out."

No, Oriana's time seemed to be forever. Estelle saw the ageless face, its skin waxy white, the wet lips that glistened. Her legs were shaking as she climbed the hill to Le Refuge, her confidence washed away by Pierre Gosselin's desperate plea, his threat of violence to come.

As she looked into that vortex of violence, she wondered if she should free herself from the crazy notion of loving Léon de Polnay. Even as the thought came to her, she knew he was at the center of her. She could not more pluck him out or wish him harm than she could her unborn child. Maybe, she thought, it's the snare that holds so many women, but my whole body sings with it. I could yoke a hundred oxen across my shoulders and pull them up Constitution Steps without pausing for breath. For the love of Léon de Polnay.

Chapter Thirty-one

THE LAST DAY OF OCTOBER. All Hallows Eve, when the power of the witch rides the highest as the nights grow darker and colder, and the warmth of summer is only a memory. Pierre Gosselin's words came back to Estelle as evening fell and the lights came on in Saint Peter Port. Would Léon's men harm Oriana, she wondered, when the fear was most upon them?

The dawn broke on a cold gray first of November, and as the day passed she wondered at her own superstitious hysteria. The men had muttered against her, but that had been the extent of their rebellion. Just as Pierre Gosselin had conveniently forgotten his hostility toward Estelle when he had wanted her help, they would forget about Oriana as November fifth approached. That was Boudlo night, an excuse to get drunk and parade through the countryside. The custom had been brought to the island earlier in the century by English immigrants, who had missed their own Guy Fawkes celebration on November fifth, when the effigy of the man who had tried to blow up Parliament was burned on a bonfire.

Estelle had always been frightened by the riotous destruction of the effigy, the Boudlo, on the great bonfires. As a child she had watched it paraded through the streets in an open carriage, surrounded by men in costume, some dressed as women. She had run away and hidden when the celebrants came knocking on the door for alms. She had never been allowed to attend the ceremonies because of the drinking and general rowdiness.

The cold gray morning of November fifth turned into afternoon without any discernible change in the light. The fire and the lamps were lit early in the salon. Celestine was in the kitchen making pies while Estelle sat sewing. The smell of hot apple and spices drifted toward her and made her think of Christmas. She smiled to herself, turning the small nightgown around in her hands. How easy it was to forget, sitting behind the walls that had shielded her childhood. Paradise regained, she thought, for she had been perfectly happy in those days.

There was a sudden outburst of sound in the hallway outside the salon, of voices raised in protest and footsteps approaching the door. It burst open unceremoniously to reveal old Luc and Celestine, still arguing.

"You'll not disturb her, I forbid it! What is it to her if the whole crew is taken to the gallows? Leave her in peace!"

Estelle's voice cut through the altercation. "No, Celestine. Let Luc tell me what has happened."

Luc hobbled in, pushing Celestine to one side in an uncharacteristically aggressive gesture. "*Princesse,* you are to come immediately. Léon de Polnay sent a message to me to take you to Michel Priaulx."

Estelle shook her head, but Celestine's relief was short-lived when she heard the answer. "No, too slow. Get me one of oncle Matthieu's horses, Luc. It won't be really dark for a while yet."

Celestine's wails of protest filled the air, pursuing Estelle down the corridor and up the stairs. From the back of her closet, Estelle pulled a heavy woollen riding-habit she hadn't worn in years.

When she came downstairs again, Celestine was standing in the hall wringing her hands and gazing agonizedly at her charge. "Think of the little one, Estelle. Imagine what could happen if you go horseback riding over the countryside?"

"Uncle William once told me my mother rode to hounds until just before I was born. It was one of the few things he remembered about her."

"But, *ma petite,* she died — God rest her soul!" wailed Celestine.

"She died of childbed fever, not from hunting, Celestine. Neither will I, although our quarry is very different." What quarry, Estelle wondered, surprised at her own reply. I haven't even asked Luc what he knows.

Luc was waiting at the stables alongside the main house, where her uncle still kept a couple of horses. Estelle took the reins from him, automatically stroking the gray mare's muzzle, checking the stirrup length. "Do you know anything more about what has happened, Luc?"

"Only that the men have done something with the one who is there — I don't know what. Monsieur Léon needs to know from you about that one, before he knows what to do."

Either old Luc's memory was befuddled or that was the way it had been told to him. There was nothing to be gained in asking any more questions. The old man helped her mount.

Estelle bent down and touched his shoulder. "Celestine must tell no one, Luc, you understand? Tell her it could be very dangerous for me if she tries."

There were already many people about. Carts and carriages jostled down the narrow streets. Many of their occupants seemed to have started celebrating already. The normally staid atmosphere of Saint Peter Port echoed with uninhibited cries.

In the countryside it was quieter, but there were still more carts and horses than usual. Most people glanced at her curiously, nodded, and went about their business. At the top of the hill overlooking le clos de Polnay, Estelle stopped her horse and looked down at the house in the valley.

There were no outward signs to indicate anything unusual. As before, smoke curled up from a chimney, blowing inland across the valley. As she watched, there was movement at the front of the house. Someone opened the door and came out, standing just over the threshold.

It was Léon, with Ranulph at his side. She could see them watching her. Their eyes never left her as she came toward them, down the long pathway and into the courtyard before the house. Estelle looked down from her horse into Léon's face. It was just as she remembered it. She smiled at him, with great sweetness, a certain gravity.

"You know," she said, "you really are too handsome to be true, Léon. You have the face that young girls dream of, so I wondered if I had made you up."

There was none of the usual mockery or laughter in his eyes when he spoke. "I was mad. *J'étais fou.*"

Estelle dismounted and put out her hand. "Tell me why I am here," was her reply.

Taking her by the hand, Léon led her into the front room, which was full of people. Pierre Gosselin was there beneath the unlit crasset lamp, with about five or six other men. The fire in the great fireplace had burned low and was mostly gray ash, as if no one had bothered with it for a long time. In front of it crouched a young lad of about sixteen or seventeen years of age, his hands on his thighs, rubbing the rough cloth of his britches as though he would put out a fire that burned on his palms. As they came in, he turned round. Estelle saw that he was weeping; from the look of his eyes he had probably been weeping for hours. They all looked at her now, eyes fastened on her as she came toward them.

Seated on the *lit de fouaille* was a figure, dressed in white, whose eyes also stared at her. For a moment, Estelle thought it was midsummer's eve, not Boudlo night, and that the silent one — la Môme — was sitting amid fern and flowers to welcome her. At the height of the summer solstice that's what one would find: a young girl, dressed for the goddess, the mute one, accepting their obeisance.

This one was mute but not a goddess, nor a young girl. She

sat there with a knife handle visible at the base of her neck, the scarlet column of blood now beginning to dry on the white silk of her dress.

Oriana.

Estelle tore her eyes from the figure and looked at Pierre Gosselin. There was silence in the room, broken only by the sobbing of the young boy. Gosselin nodded. "I told you how it would be," he said. Around him, the men stirred and sighed, as if with one breath. Estelle had the feeling they had all been here, like this, a very long time.

Behind her, Léon said, "They will tell me nothing."

Pierre Gosselin spoke again. "We all did it. We had planned to do it tonight. Burn her like the witch she is. He —" he pointed at the boy "— told her, warned her, and she laughed at him. But it was when she told him why she didn't believe we would, that she had been with all of us, that he did it. It was a filthy lie, but it gave her pleasure to taunt the poor young fool. I am telling you all this, madame, but I'll deny every word outside this room. It's not right that an innocent should be punished for her, since we would all have killed her tonight. We are all guilty."

She heard Léon groan behind her. "*Crétin,* why wouldn't you tell me?"

Before Pierre Gosselin could answer, Estelle asked a question of her own. "How would you have done it tonight?"

"She drinks like a fish, so we would have drunk with her and then taken her with us. She would have been our Boudlo. We would have said it was an accident, that she had fallen into the fire. It has happened. Not to the death, but it has happened."

Oriana had driven them all mad: Léon, Pierre, Paul, the rest of them. She guessed they hadn't told Léon, because they blamed him for what had happened. She, too, was guilty in their eyes. They all were, everyone in the room.

Oriana, most of all. Pierre Gosselin was right. It would not be justice to see a seventeen-year-old hang for such an act. Estelle looked again at Oriana, who appeared to be laughing, even in death. It was an illusion, but it renewed Estelle's loathing as she felt the old fears rising in her. She closed her eyes, swayed, and felt Léon hold her around the waist.

His voice carried over her head in anger. "Now that you have told her, maybe I can do something!" He turned Estelle to face him, his voice now gentle. "Are there people in England or France who would pursue the truth of this matter, if we continue with what they had originally planned?"

There was another groundswell of sound from the men in the room, as they took in what Léon was saying.

"I think it unlikely any verdict would be questioned from there, if you can persuade the authorities here. She came here because she said she had nowhere else to go. I think that's probably true."

"Very well, we'll do it tonight as they planned. Easier to explain an accident with a bonfire, than a knife wound in the throat. The fire will clear away the evidence for us."

There was another murmur and Pierre Gosselin looked around at the other men. "Come," he said. "We go to build a bonfire. Paul, go home to your mother. Tell her you are ill, tell her you had a fight with me, tell her what you wish, but do not tell her the truth. Say nothing to anyone ever, for the rest of your life, or every single person in this room is in jeopardy."

Gosselin pulled the youngster to his feet and pushed him toward the door. As the men moved in a group around the *lit de fouaille*, Estelle turned and for the last time walked away from Oriana.

They have killed her, she thought. They will burn her body tonight. They would have burned her alive. She was astonished that she was not appalled. An eye for an eye, a tooth for a tooth — how deep that must go.

Outside the bedroom window, beyond the closed curtains, the light suddenly sprang up, turning the room to amber and gold. There was a roaring sound, a cacophony of voices. Estelle got up from the bed on which she had been lying and went over to the window, pulling the curtains back with both hands.

The men were dancing. Faces blackened for the burning of the Boudlo, they leaped and shrieked around the great bonfire, laughter crackling and spitting with the flames in the night air. There was no self-doubt, no agony of remorse for them, either.

In the blazing heart of the fire, a blackened, twisted thing moved and danced in its turn, and the men bowed and saluted it, mocking partners in this grotesque quadrille of death.

Behind her, the door opened quietly, as if whoever opened it did not wish to disturb the sleeper inside.

"Come away from the window, Estelle. You shouldn't be there." Léon was in a heavy Guernsey sweater and dark trousers, and he had removed his shoes so as not to wake her.

Carefully Estelle closed the curtains over the window again. "I wanted to know she was really dead."

Léon's laugh was short, unamused. "The men say I'll need a silver bullet for that. Myself, I think a knife-blade and a fire should suffice."

"So do I, for I have decided not to believe in witches any more. You were just weak, *mon homme,* and so was I. It's too easy to blame it on Oriana."

Léon knelt by the empty bed and rested his head in his hands, rubbing his eyes as though they stung him. "Maybe so. But *Dieu,* Estelle, what possessed me? How could I have gone on when I knew Florian was gone? That you loved me? I am more despicable than even *I* thought I was!"

"Because, in my own way, I frightened you quite as much as Oriana. And I imagine she worked on the jealousy you already felt. Florian became part of my life because I wanted to punish Cosimo and Oriana, but I think I may also have wanted to punish you."

"You succeeded, *petite étoile,* beyond your wildest dreams."

With her back to the glow from the window, Léon couldn't see her face, but she brought her arms across her body, as if hugging some secret to herself. Léon remembered when Oriana lay revealed before him and marvelled that the same gesture could be so different. In this movement he read triumph, yes, but also laughter and love.

"Are you laughing at me, Estelle?"

"It just occurred to me that you are leaning on what should have been our marriage bed, Léon de Polnay."

He extended his hands across the bed toward her. It was an unusually tentative gesture, as if he were afraid of frightening her away.

"This is perhaps not the time to say it, but it could be still, Estelle, if you can bring yourself to want me again."

She sounded severe as she came nearer, her hands still clasped around her elbows, her body straight. But as her face emerged from the shadows he saw she was smiling. "It is the time to say it, Léon, and should have been said already. I am carrying your child, who will be born in the spring."

Léon's handsome face was not radiant or joyful or romantic. He gaped at her, jaw dropped, thunderstruck.

"What? When?"

She knelt on the other side of the bed and took his hands in hers. "What do you mean, when? You know precisely when. Once and once only, Léon, and . . . you gave me a child."

He was on the bed, pulling her up against him, hugging her, kissing her. She felt tears on her lips and on her cheeks.

"Softly, my darling. Are you so pleased to be trapped into this marriage bed? Ah, Léon!"

What better way, she thought, as she heard her own cry, felt his calloused seaman's hands on her breasts. What better way to exorcise the cataclysmic past than to hold this man whom she loved in such a release of passion that she felt it explode in the depths of her body as she had never felt it before, not even when he had come to Le Refuge and given her a child. Then, there had been talking to do and the knowledge — only half-understood on her part — that someone else lay between them. The words came afterward.

"Will you marry me, Estelle Gastineau?"

"What a question to ask a woman on her marriage bed, de Polnay. You married me this summer, remember?"

"Ah, was that what I did, Madame de Polnay. However, I would still like to hear your answer."

Sitting there in the glow from the window, pearl and cream and gold, her smile was mischievous and tender.

"Yes, my husband, I will marry you."

Léon de Polnay put out his hand and ran it over her full breasts, the barely perceptible curve of her stomach. "Marriage suits you. You look even more like the figurehead I have carved for the *Nerine*."

Her low laugh and half-glance, the movement of her body beneath his hand quickened his desire again.

"I'm glad you approve. This is the first time, but not the last that I'll look like this. Of that I am sure."

"And I, too." He felt pride in his manhood, a sense of fulfillment and accomplishment he had not found before in the merely sensual release he had so constantly sought, for so many years. The dark-blue eyes looked into his, and he saw her desire reflected in them, as he felt his own.

"You want me again," she said.

"Yes. And you want me."

"Yes. I love you, you see."

"I see — Oh, how I see, Estelle. I love you." There, it was so easy to say now, those words that she alone had first torn from him.

This time it was she who stopped his mouth with her kisses, as Léon started to tell her of his discovery, twining her body over and around him, her long blond hair falling like a curtain about his face as he pulled her onto him and folded her into his embrace.

The flames still leaped outside, but the two inside were the heat of the bonfire, the heart of the flame. They burned unconsumed, paradise regained. They made love until they could no longer see the flames dancing on the ceiling, until a brief darkness fell before the dawn came.

Just before she fell asleep, Estelle felt Léon's hand move gently across her body. He left it there, curved protectively over the child he had given her in answer to a letter.

Chapter Thirty-two

THE PATH TO THE CHURCH of Saint Martin's was strewn with rushes and late-blooming autumn flowers. As she passed with Léon de Polnay through the gates, Estelle paused and looked at la Gran'mère du Chimquière. She took a flower from her bouquet and laid it at her feet. "*Merci,* madame," she whispered, looking into the broad, peaceful face.

The house had been decorated outside with flags and bunting and Chinese lanterns. Marie Priaulx and Celestine had been up early to bake the hams, hotpots, cakes, and crepes in the great furze oven. There was mulled wine, cider, and grander libations from the great cellars of the de Polnay farm and Le Refuge. Michel Priaulx had brought his *chiffournie*, the old country accordion, for the dancing. The young men of the parish standing outside the gates cheering and firing their militia muskets were invited inside to drink mulled wine and cider and to join in the celebration.

All were welcome, for Léon de Polnay was finally getting married — and to the right girl. It was years since their *fiançailles.* Long overdue, said everyone, nodding wisely. There had been that terrible business about the mad Englishwoman drinking and falling into the fire. Everyone had been so concerned Léon would feel obligated to make an honest woman out of her. Even her ashes had been sent back to the mainland, for she didn't belong here with her heathen ways, they all said, touching their amulets for luck.

All that was forgotten now, as they raised the rafters with laughter and song and toasted the bridal couple. Pierre Gosselin was a happy man, for he had been put in charge of the *Nerine* so that Léon de Polnay could stay on the island and supervise the building of his new ship at Saint Sampson. He was now getting involved in the running of ballast, coal, and granite between England, France, and Guernsey. It was not as romantic as running brandy or tobacco but more fitting for the head of the household, *le père de famille*. And quite as lucrative, for Léon de Polnay was as clever a businessman as he had been a buccaneer.

In early May, when the islanders drink milk-à-punch to welcome the arrival of Beltainn, the sun god, their daughter was born. Her lusty cries rang through the house in the clos de Polnay like the voices of the guests at her parents' wedding only six months before. The islanders tutted, shook their heads and said, "He's a chip off the old block, that one," then winked an eye and wet the baby's head with more *milk-à-punch*.

"Dark hair and flashing eyes, just like her father. *Petite fleur*."

"I'm amazed, because I was so sure she would be like you, *ma blonde étoile*."

"We will have a son that looks like me. Don't ask me how I know that, but I do. But neither will *be* like me. They will be much wiser."

"Hush. All we can do is hope to give them the strength to live their lives. And love."

"Ah yes, love. Love is stronger than a hundred oxen."

"We are so practical, we islanders. We even make love work for us."

Eyelashes curved against a perfectly rounded cheek, tiny

fingers curling round his great calloused index finger, filling him with a passion different from but as profound as the one Léon felt for her mother. How could he have been afraid to be caught by such a marvel as this? Léon de Polnay looked at the beautiful face of his wife against the embroidered pillows, felt the mixture of desire and delight she always inspired in him.

"Some snares," he mused out loud, "are only there for us if we are clever enough to fall into them. Oh —" He patted his pocket, suddenly remembering. "This came for you."

It was a very small package. Inside the wrapping was a dark-blue velvet box, satin-lined. Estelle opened it and found a star of diamonds on a gold chain.

"*Dieu!*" exclaimed Léon, astonished. "Who gave you such a gift, Estelle?"

Estelle didn't answer him at once. She was unfolding the slip of paper that lay over the diamond star. After reading it silently she handed it to Léon, and he read it out loud:

> "At night, when I see unveiled in the sky
> the golden stars, my heart dreams of you;
> By day, beautiful young girl with the gentle glance,
> when I see you, I think of the stars."

The note was signed "Olympio."

"Who is he, Olympio?" asked Léon.

Estelle looked at her husband. "An immortal," she replied. She gazed at her daughter in Léon's arms, and her eyes swam with unshed tears.

Historical Note

Victor Hugo: French poet of the Romantic school, who was exiled in Guernsey for his opposition to Emperor Napoleon III between 1855 and 1873.

La nuit, quand je vois dans les cieux sans voiles
les étoiles d'or, mon coeur songe à vous;
Le jour, jeune belle aux regards si doux,
lorsque je vous vois, je songe aux étoiles.

These lines from Victor Hugo's madrigal were not written for Estelle. But they might have been.

La Roque Varou: There are many ancient standing stones — menhirs and dolmens — on Guernsey, such as la Gran'mère du Chimquière, but la Roque Varou is a figment of my imagination. The werewolf, however, is indeed part of island mythology.

JILL DOWNIE

ANGEL IN BABYLON

A story of ambition, intrigue and love set in the glittering world of the Victorian theatre.

Lured by the beckoning lights of the London stage, Serena Whitcome defied convention to pursue her dream.

Life in Drury Lane was intoxicating to Serena. She tasted heady success in the theatre and savoured the passionate attentions of countless admirers. If the disturbing presence of a handsome volatile actor, Nicholas Mackenzie, raised deeper longings, she sternly ignored them.

But corrupt predators prowled the fringes of her bright life. And when the sadistic desires of Viscount Hector Percival threaten to destroy not only Serena but the one man she cares for, she sees the desperate fragility of her way of life . . .

NORMA HARRIS

THE DANCE MASTER

Dorsey, *Shane* and *Alexandra*, the dancers.

On stage they are all grace and energy, seemingly effortless, almost lighter than air.

Back stage and in rehearsal there is real blood, real sweat and real tears as minds and bodies are strained to breaking point.

Driving them on, always demanding more is Caligari, the dance master, the man with his own dream: the creation of his own ballet company. The man with a vision for which he will drive both himself and his dancers with a ruthless passion.

Dorsey, *Shane* and *Alexandra*, each with her ambitions, her secret fears, her physical and emotional needs. And Caligari, who can make or break each one of them.

NEW ENGLISH LIBRARY